MEMOIRS OF A REVOLUTIONARY

Upendra Nath Banerjee

MEMOIRS OF A REVOLUTIONARY

Upendra Nath Banerjee

EDITED BY
ANIRBAN GANGULY

Vitasta

Published by
Vitasta Publishing Pvt Ltd
2/15, Ansari Road, Daryaganj
New Delhi-110 002
info@vitastapublishing.com

ISBN 978-81-963329-5-2
© Anirban Ganguly
Reprint Edition 2023
First Published by K.L.Chakravarty, Calcutta circa 1924
MRP ₹ 399

All Rights Reserved.
No part of this publication may be reproduced, stored in a retrieval system, or transmitted in any form, or by any means—electronic, mechanical, photocopying, recording or otherwise—without the prior permission of the publisher. Opinions expressed in this book are the author's own. The publisher is in no way responsible for these.

Cover and Layout by Somesh Kumar Mishra
Printed by Chaman Enterprises, New Delhi

CONTENTS

Foreword......vii
Publisher note......xv
Acknowledgments......xvii
Introduction...... xix

CHAPTER I......1
CHAPTER II...... 10
CHAPTER III...... 19
CHAPTER IV...... 30
CHAPTER V......37
CHAPTER VI......46
CHAPTER VII......54
CHAPTER VIII...... 61
CHAPTER IX......68
CHAPTER X...... 75
CHAPTER XI...... 85
CHAPTER XII......96
CHAPTER XIII...... 101
CHAPTER XIV......110

Glossary...... *119*
Maniktaula Garden House Revolutionaries...... *134*

FOREWORD

MEMOIRS OF a Revolutionary—Indeed, Upendranath Bandyopadhyay (also written as Upendra Nath Banerjee) was a revolutionary and much more. He was born in Chandannagar (Hooghly) on 6th June 1879 and died on 4th April 1950. In 1908, there was a famous trial, formally known as 'Emperor versus Aurobindo Ghosh and Others'. The judgement was delivered in 1909 by CP Beachcroft. Though that is the formal name of the case, popularly the case is known as the Alipore Bomb Case, the Muraripukur Conspiracy, or the Manicktolla Bomb Conspiracy. The trial took place in the Alipore Sessions Court and the accused were picked up from 32, Muraripukur Road in Manicktolla.

The charge was: 'That you, on or about the 12 months preceding May 15th, 1908, at various places in Bengal including 32, Muraripukur Road, Maniktola of...' '... *waging war against His Majesty the King-Emperor of India* ...' '... *conspiring to deprive His Majesty the King-Emperor of India of the Sovereignty of British India or a part thereof* ...' '... *to overawe by criminal force the Government of India or the Local Government of India* ...'... and thereby, committed an offence punishable under Section 121 of the Indian Penal Code, and within the cognizance of the Court of Sessions.' It was not just Section 121 of IPC (Indian Penal Code), but Sections 121A and 122 too. Those sections of IPC, with suitable amendments, still exist. At that time, it was a question of 'waging war' against the 'Emperor' and instead of "imprisonment for life', there was 'transportation for life'. Instead of a fine, there was 'forfeiture of all property'. There were 37 prisoners on trial.

Where would they be transported for life? To the Cellular Jail in Port Blair, now a national monument. Though the origins can be traced back to 1857, the 'Kala-Pani' prison specifically earmarked for freedom-fighters, was constructed in the last decade of the 19th century and was ready by 1906. A few of the original seven wings still remain. Visitors can get a sense of what prison life was like, though it is impossible to fathom the cruelty of David Barrie (also spelt as Barry), the jailor of the Cellular Jail between 1905 and 1919. In the list of political prisoners who were sent to the Andamans, Bengal and Punjab featured prominently. Upendra Nath Banerjee was among the first batch of political prisoners.

The background to the trial was the aborted partition of Bengal in 1905 and the stimulus this gave to the nationalist movement. The background was the formation of Anushilan Samiti (1902) and Jugantar (1907), more importantly, Manicktola Secret Society in 1907, of which, Upendra Nath Banerjee was a member. In 1907, there were failed attempts to assassinate Andrew Fraser (Lieutenant Governor of Bengal) and L Tardivel (Mayor of Chandannagar). The background was also Muzaffarpur, when in April 1908, Khudiram Bose and Prafulla Chaki

hurled a bomb at what they thought was the carriage of Douglas Kingsford, the magistrate. Instead, two British ladies (wife and daughter of Pringle Kennedy) were killed. Fearing apprehension, Prafulla Chaki killed himself and Khudiram Bose was eventually hanged on 11th August 1908. A song written by Pitambar Das in Bangla is still extremely popular in Bengal, the english translation of which is as under:
O Mother! Grant me adieu once. I will return. I will smile as I wear the noose and all the residents of Bharata will look on...Abhiram has been transported to an island and Khudiram will hang.

In popular imagination, Abhiram is identified with Ullaskar Dutta (1885-1965). The raids in May 1908, leading to the Alipore Bomb Case, were in retaliation. On 2nd May 1908, fourteen people were arrested from 32, Muraripukur Road. Barindra Kumar Ghose (1880-1959), Ullaskar Dutta and Upendra Nath Banerjee were among them. In the course of the trial, Narendranath Goswami turned approver and was killed inside the Presidency Jail by Kanailal Dutta and Satyendranath Bose, both of them were hanged in November 2008. In the Alipore Bomb Case, Sri Aurobindo, defended by Chittaranjan Das, was acquitted, as were several others.

Barindra Kumar Ghose and Ullaskar Dutta were sentenced to be hanged. On appeal, this was commuted to transportation for life. Along with several others, Upendra Nath Banerjee was also sentenced to transportation for life. After being interred in Alipore Presidency Jail during the period of trial, he was sent to the Cellular Jail in January 1910 and released in late December

1919 or early 1920. Those are the bare facts.

This book is not the only one of Upendra Nath Banerjee's works. Post release from the Andaman Cellular Jail, he wrote regularly for magazines/newspapers such as *Narayan*, *Bijali*, *Banglar Katha*, *Forward*, *Udbhodan* and *Kheyali*. He wrote for and edited *Atmashakti* and *Dainik Basumati*, and also wrote for *Liberty* and *Amrita Bazar Patrika*. (In between, from 1923 to 1926, he was imprisoned again in Alipore Jail.) Other than the present volume, he is the author of several Bengali books *Unapanchashi* (Forty-Nine), *Pather Sandhan* (In search of the Path), *Anantander Patra* (Anantananda's letter), *Svadhin Manush* (The independent man), *Bartaman Samasya* (The Present Crisis), *Jater Birambana* (Embarrassment of *Jati*), *Sinn Fein*, *Dharma-Karma* and *Bhabaghurer Chithi* (A Nomad's Letter). Except the last three, the others have been reprinted in Bengali some six years ago. They have probably not been translated into English.

To gauge the thoughts, philosophy, humour and quality of Upendra Nath Banerjee's prose, one has to read these too. Indeed, the quality of prose is impossible to capture in any translation, including the present one. For example, *Memoirs of a Revolutionary* is a misnomer. In Bengali, the book was titled নির্বাসিতের আত্মকথা, *Nirbasiter Atmakatha*. 'Memoirs' is acceptable for 'Atmakatha'. But there is no 'Revolutionary' in the Bengali title. A proper English translation would have been 'Memoirs of an Exile'. Though this wouldn't have captured Upendra Nath Banerjee's role in the freedom movement, I happen to think this is much more poignant.

Why was *Nirbasiter Atmakatha* so successful when it was published? For a start, at that time little was known about the penal colony in Cellular Jail. Such severe were the restrictions that little information went in and little came out. As a fall-out of the Indian Jails Committee of 1919-20, reports and resentment started surfacing in the 1920s. Second, the perception was that the Cellular Jail was meant for murderers and those guilty of serious crimes against person and property, not PLUs (People like us), Bengali middle class freedom-fighters who were subjected to the same harsh and penal conditions. *Nirbasiter Atmakatha* was serialised in *Narayan* in 1921 and published the same year (By Arya Publishing House) as a book.

Barindra Kumar Ghosh also wrote about his experiences in *Dvipantarer Pathe* (The Path to Transportation, serialised from 1922), 'Boma Yuger Kahini' (The story of the period of bombs, serialised from 1922), *Dvipantarer Katha* (The Story of Transportation, published in the 1920s), *Amar Atmakatha* (My Memoirs, reprinted in 1931, published in English as *The Tale of My Exile*). But these were memoirs, in a class different from that of Upendra Nath Banerjee's.

Ullaskar Dutta also wrote about his experiences in Amar Karajiban, translated into English as Twelve Years of Prison Life and published in 1924. But Ullaskar Dutta lost his mental balance in Andaman and thus, large parts of this memoir are hallucinatory. After an amendment to the Indian Press Act in 1922, it became easier to publish such accounts. This included the 1923 book by Nalinikishor Guha, *Banglay Biplab-bad* (Revolutionary Movements in Bengal).

Veer Savarkar's account of transportation was published a little later between 1925 and 1927, it was originally written in Marathi. Upendra Nath Banerjee's was the first such account. Third, there is the quality of prose which is why it appealed so much to the likes of Rabindranath Tagore, Syed Mujtaba Ali, Sarala Devi Chaudhurani and numerous other readers. His is a matter-of-fact style, devoid of emotions, with a wry sense of humour, despite the hardships he had been through. There is a capacity to laugh at oneself and not take oneself too seriously.

How does one send such harrowing tales? He left his son when the child was just one and a half years old and when he returned the boy was thirteen. The Bengali reads far better. Here is the English translation, the conclusion, 'O my God, thou sittest at the helm of Life and Death, whither wouldst thou lead me on this time?' Not a trace of bitterness. Or sample this. 'The bare idea that I would be sitting idly at my fireside while others were liberating India behind my back was too much for me.' Alternatively, 'Even a few unknown faces caught mine eyes. Where did the misery hail from?'

I asked one of them, 'Who are you, my dear fellow?' He whined out, 'I live at Manicktala, Sir. I went for a morning walk into the neighbourhood of your gardens, but the Police got hold of me. I had no idea that morning walks could bring one within the limits of the Penal Code.' Cellular Jail was much more than traumatic. Unable to bear the torture, young Indu Bhushan Roy committed suicide. Ullaskar Dutta lost his mental balance. To write all this with such equanimity and poise is nothing short of remarkable.

These are the forgotten pages of India's history. These are the forgotten pages of Bengal's history. There is an Upendra Nath Banerjee Road in Kolkata, but I doubt very much whether those who pass are aware of who Upendra Nath Banerjee was. (A statue was unveiled recently, on 11th December 2021). I congratulate Dr Anirban Ganguly, who also happens to be

Upendra Nath Banerjee's great great grandson, for taking interest in bringing these forgotten pages of history to the attention of the present generation and for republishing an account by a remarkable individual, author and freedom fighter.

January 2023

Bibek Debroy
Indologist and Chairman,
Economic Advisory Council
to Government of India

PUBLISHER NOTE

OVER THE past decade, Vitasta has had the privilege of presenting several meticulously researched stories, chronicling the lives of the unsung heroes of our freedom struggle. We have strived to bring these remarkable stories to our readers, shedding light on the contributions of individuals who have largely been ignored

Today as we are celebrating the 75th year of India's Independence, we take immense pride in republishing the *Memoirs of a Revolutionary* written by a remarkable individual and freedom fighter, Upendra Nath Banerjee. His unparalleled dedication to India's freedom struggle has remained overshadowed and overlooked for far too long.

Throughout time, the sacrifices made by our heroes have been eclipsed by more dominant historical narratives, leaving their significant contributions unrecognized. Their courage, determination and selflessness deserve and demand a greater appreciation from us, who have inherited the gift of a free India. It is essential that the younger generation is made aware of the sacrifices of these extraordinary individuals. The struggles they faced, the risks they undertook, and the unwavering spirit they embodied should not be forgotten .

As you delve into the pages of this book you may come across a language that appears archaic by today's standards. It is important to note that this deliberate decision was made to preserve the authenticity of the memoirs in its original form. By presenting the book as it was intended, we offer readers a glimpse into the era that shaped the revolutionary and the nation.

We hope that this publication serves as a fitting tribute to one of the greatest revolutionaries our country has produced. May it ignite a sense of reverence and appreciation for the unsung heroes who dedicated their lives to the cause of India's independence. Let their stories inspire us to cherish and protect the freedom for which they fought so valiantly.

ACKNOWLEDGMENTS

I WOULD like to express my gratitude to Professor Bibek Debroy, author, thinker, polymath and Chairman of the Prime Minister's Economic Advisory Council (PM-EAC) for penning an inspiring foreword to the work. Amidst his heavy responsibilities he has unfailingly found time, over the years, to encourage and to support my work.

I am thankful to Sri Aurobindo Ashram Archives at Puducherry for lending me a copy of the original copy of the English translation of Upendra Nath Banerjee's "Nirbasiter Atmakatha" and for sharing photographs of the Maniktollah revolutionaries.

I thank Biresh Chaudhuri, Suman Bhowmik of Sutradhar, Kolkata, Amit Kumar and Shailendra Shukla for their help in preparing the manuscript.

I thank Smt Renu Kaul Verma of Vitasta Publications for showing interest in the work and for bringing it out in record time.

My gratitude to my wife Smt Anuttama Ganguly, Secretary, Vivekananda International Foundation (VIF) for her constant support and encouragement and for her firm conviction that the saga of forgotten revolutionaries must be unearthed, preserved and narrated for posterity.

INTRODUCTION
Revolutionary & Thinker
Upendra Nath Banerjee

ADDRESSING THE centenary celebration of Nagaland's and the Northeast's iconic freedom fighter and spiritual leader Rani Gaidinliu (1915-1993) in August 2015, Prime Minister Narendra Modi had observed that "either we have forgotten such great people or we have been made to forget on purpose."[1]

It is one of the tragedies of our freedom movement's narrative that contributions and memories of a large number of freedom fighters who took part and led India's struggle for independence in their region and suffered great privations for it, were swept into oblivion once freedom was attained.

Speaking at a book release function in New Delhi in January 2023, India's Home Minister Amit Shah, himself a keen student and scholar of history, argued that though the British had left India history continued to be written through their prism. Shah argued that the narrative of armed struggle in India's independence was given short shrift and was neglected.

---

1 Anirban Ganguly, 'Widening the Narrative', *The Millennium Post*, 16 November 2021.

The prevalent narrative that there was no role of an armed struggle in India's freedom was not correct. Shah pointed out that this was argued by historians whose narratives of India's freedom struggle were suppressed. He said that had armed struggles not taken place it would have taken India many more years to achieve her independence.

In November 2022, speaking at the conclusion of a grand celebration of the legacy of Assam's iconic warrior-general Lachit Borphukhan, Shah argued, 'I hear many times that our history has been misrepresented… it has been distorted. There is a possibility that what has been written was right, but who can stop us now from rewriting our history with pride? We will have to amend this and put our history in front of the world with pride.'[2]

Legacies of Rani Gaidinliu's contributions in the Northeast, and participation of the tea tribe community of Assam in India's freedom struggle, have all been consigned to oblivion. How can the legacy and sacrifice of Mangri Orang (Malati Mem) who was killed by the British because she participated in the non-cooperation movement, be forgotten and why could their contributions never find nation-wide acceptance or documentation? In the early years of independence, the effort to put together a comprehensive narrative of the freedom movement was still-born because of political pressures by the

---

2 'No One Can Stop India from rewriting its history: Amit Shah', *Hindustan Times*, November 22, 2021.

Nehruvian establishment to make it unidirectional, unilateral and narrowly focused.[3]

In a foreword to a Bengali book on the revolutionary Jatindranath Mukherjee – Bagha Jatin – '*Biplabi Jatindranath*', that appeared in August 1947, Dr Syama Prasad Mookerjee pleaded for initiating a systematic and comprehensive detailing of the lives and contributions of the forgotten freedom fighters of India. 'These youthful revolutionaries', wrote Syama Prasad, 'had forsaken and given up all they had and plunged in the fire of revolution. By sacrificing themselves cell by cell they gave a taste of the greater life of freedom that awaited us. Yet today they have been forgotten, today's youth has no idea of their contributions or their names. Their heroic exploits have not been recorded in the pages of history either here or abroad. The fear of state oppression, the apprehensions of generating negative public opinion and the sense of being correct had for long withheld the pens of historians' from undertaking such a work. [Translated from Bengali]

Apart from Rani Gaidinliu, the other personality who experienced a similar fate was Subramania Bharati (1882-1921), the '*Maha Kavi*' of the revolutionary movement. To

---

3 Appendix to the first volume of RC Majumdar's three volume opus, 'History of the Freedom Movement in India, (1962)', for a firsthand account of how the Nehru establishment scuttled the effort to write an authentic history of the freedom movement. 'Ever since the achievement of independence on 15th August, 1947,' began Majumdar, 'the idea possessed me that steps should be taken for compiling a history of India's struggle for freedom. I accordingly moved a Resolution to that effect in the Jaipur Session of the Indian Historical Records Commission held in February, 1948.' Majumdar's resolution said, 'that an attempt be made to compile a list of important records, both published and unpublished, bearing upon the national struggle for freedom.'

deliver justice and recognition to a forgotten great, it took a historic gesture by Prime Minister Modi to institute a Chair in the epochal poet's name at Banaras Hindu University on the centenary of the Maha Kavi's passing (11th September 2021). It gave the quest for an authentic and all-encompassing narrative of the freedom movement a major fillip and, in a sense, linked the legacy of the freedom struggle in the South with that in Northern India.

For political and ideological reasons, their legacies faced marginalisation or were only paid lip service. No concrete or substantial initiative was launched to preserve and disseminate their contributions, or to comprehensively integrate them in the broader narrative of the freedom movement. Often, the regional variations and contributions were neglected or minimised. Even when they were considered, as has been done by a section of Communist historians, it was with the intention of delinking them from the larger flow, of placing them as leaders who had no sense of the whole, and therefore, ideal icons whose legacies could be pushed to present the narrative of national fragmentation.

This sweeping aside was a motivated political and ideological move to try and dilute the nationalist core of our struggle for independence. Such has been the fate of a large number of revolutionaries across India.

Prime Minister Narendra Modi's declaration of observing November 15, the birth anniversary of the iconic Adivasi, spiritual and social leader, and freedom fighter Bhagawan Birsa Munda as '*Janajatiya Gaurav Divas*', addresses a vast lacunae in the narrative of our freedom movement. The decision to establish tribal museums in various parts of the country and to encourage the dissemination of their legacy of participation in India's freedom movement is in itself a very crucial step in integrating this long neglected aspect. It cements the intellectual and physical contributions of Janajati leaders thus, reigniting the India narrative. All these leaders were also active social reformers and educators, and freedom for them consisted of social empowerment and the spread of education.

Many of whose legacies have been side-lined, were driven and inspired by the deeper dimensions of the struggle – which was cultural and spiritual. Many struggled to broaden the movement and include the masses, the subalterns and the disempowered. A number of them churned out writings, launched dailies, edited papers and journals that disseminated revolutionary thought, laid the ideational foundation and developed the arguments for freedom. Eventually, these became widely popular among the intelligentsia and the masses. Most of these revolutionaries were also clear that freedom must be complete and absolute. Self-government within the 'Empire' was not an option for India, they argued. Freedom had to be unconditional and reflected through complete severance from the colonial and imperial link.

That the new nationalism must be expansive, broad-based and comprehensive was clearly understood by these revolutionaries. The attempt to paint them as isolationists, marginal and representing the fringe – as has been done by a section since independence – must be seen with scepticism.

Sri Aurobindo (1872-1950), writing on the awakening of the new nationalism in India spoke of such a widening. Describing the new nationalism, Sri Aurobindo wrote in 1908:

> ...overleaps every barrier; it calls to the clerk at his counter, the trader in his shop, the peasant at his plough; it summons the Brahmin from his temple and

takes the hand [of] the Chandala in his degradation; it seeks out the student in his college, the schoolboy at his books, it touches the very child in its mother's arms and the secluded zenana has thrilled to its voice; its eye searches the jungle for the Santal and travels the hills for the wild tribes of the mountains. It cares nothing for age or sex or caste or wealth or education or respectability... It cries to all to come forth, to help in God's work and remake a nation, each with what his creed or his culture, his strength, his manhood or his genius can give to the new nationality.

Most of these forgotten revolutionaries were driven and inspired by the vision of India's cultural recovery. The vision of a free India not only from political subjection, but also free to express her cultural aspirations, pushed these revolutionaries to articulate the cultural dimension through their writings and by founding institutions and encouraging young scholars to undertake study and research from the Indian perspective. They were inspired by some of India's most well-known cultural thinkers, who were either their contemporaries or near contemporaries and who spoke of the return to India's cultural and civilisational roots, which would lead to an all-round awakening from degeneration caused by political subjugation.

Of these avant-garde cultural thinkers, philosopher Ram Swarup (1920-1998) wrote that when India's freedom was a distant goal and when those who spoke of it referred to the need to 'frankly accept the British connection as ordained, in the inscrutable dispensation of providence, for India's good'. These great cultural thinkers 'who were also great *sadhakas* arose and spoke of their cultural heritage, about Vedas, about

Sanatana Dharma, with pride.' These thinkers and seers also 'gave Western culture a closer look and found it wanting in deeper matters.'

Sri Aurobindo expressed this best when he wrote, 'We reject the claim of aliens to force upon us a civilisation inferior to our own or to keep us out of our inheritance on the untenable ground of a superior fitness.'

Copies of Swami Vivekananda's speeches delivered from Colombo to Almora, on his return from the West were staple reading among revolutionary nationalists. In a moving 'personal reminiscences' on Vivekananda, Nolini Kanta Gupta, one of Sri Aurobindo's chief disciples and an early revolutionary recruit at the Muraripukur Garden House who was arrested in the Alipore Bomb Case, wrote:

> A young man is in prison accused of conspiracy and waging war against the British Empire. If convicted he might have to suffer the extreme penalty, at least, transportation to the Andamans. The case is dragging on for long months. And the young man is in a solitary cell. He cannot always keep up his spirits high. Moments of sadness and gloom and despair come and almost overwhelm him. Who was there to console and cheer him up? Vivekananda. Vivekananda's speeches, *From Colombo to Almora*, came, as a godsend, into the hands of a young man. Invariably, when the period of despondency came he used to open the book, read a few pages, read them over again, and the cloud was there no longer. Instead there was hope and courage and faith and future and light and air.

Legions of revolutionaries were inspired by him and some

such as Bagha Jatin – Jatindrana Nath Mukherjee – one of the leaders of the early group of revolutionary nationalists associated with Sri Aurobindo, had direct initiation from Vivekananda and was close to Sister Nivedita. It was Vivekananda who inspired Jatindra Nath to take up the mission of freeing India. In 1898, when Jatin was in Calcutta University, the 'air of the capital', writes philosopher-historian Prithwindra Mukherjee, 'was surcharged with sayings of Swami Vivekananda.' Vivekananda urged the youth to go wherever epidemic were raging, where people were suffering or dying of famine: *'go and die for a noble cause!'* Swami Vivekananda inspired and led bands of young men to organise relief against the plague that had hit Calcutta. Jatin joined the group and displayed uncommon leadership qualities and 'Vivekananda saw this young student several times and oriented him to a constructive programme.'

Of Jatin's reverence and admiration for Vivekananda, Sister Nivedita wrote, 'A young man came to see me, who aspires to raise the youth of India in the name of the Swami [Vivekananda]. Full of admiration for the Master, himself, he is all strength.' Of Vivekananda's direction to Jatin to build physical strength, Prithwindra writes how Vivekananda sent him 'to the gymnasium of Ambu Guha' – Ambika Charan Guha – said to be the founder of the gymnasium movement in Bengal, where he had himself 'practised wrestling.' This gymnasium 'was a crossroads of great minds and leaders' and here Jatin forged crucial and lasting relationships with future revolutionaries.

Vivekananda himself had clear ideas of organising a revolution to free India. He is reported to have told one of his Western disciples Sister Christine, how he had the 'idea of forming a combination of Indian princes for the overthrow of the foreign yoke' and how for that reason he had 'tramped all over the country', from 'the Himalayas to Cape Comorin.' The Swami also became 'friends with the gun-maker Sir Hiram Maxim' – the British-American inventor of the machine gun – to effectuate a revolution, 'but I got no response from the country. The country is dead', he had lamented.

Sakharam Ganesh Deuskar (1869-1912), a Maharashtrian scholar residing in Bengal and acknowledged as an outstanding author in Bengali and a radical thinker, whose *Desher Katha* (Tales of the Country), had created a sensation during the Swadeshi era and was promptly proscribed by the British administration, recalled a dialogue he had with Swami Vivekananda in Belur. He had asked the monk of India's future and immediately came the retort, 'The country has become a powder magazine. A little spark may ignite it...' Deuskar's revelation of this conversation in 1904 galvanised the young revolutionaries.

Of Deuskar's classic, historian and author Manoj Das writes, 'first published in 1904 the book went into several reprints and sold ten thousand copies during the first three years, an unsurpassed record for a book of such serious nature. Each copy had numerous readers as the book was a must for members of the secret societies and branches of the Anushilan Samiti.' Years later in a note on his political life, Sri Aurobindo did not forget to mention Deuskar and the formidable impact his work had on the revolution and the revolutionaries:

> He [Sri Aurobindo] encouraged the young men in the centres of work to propagate the Swadeshi idea which at that time was only in its infancy and hardly more than a fad of the few. One of the ablest men in these revolutionary groups was a Mahratta named Sakharam Ganesh Deuskar, who was an able writer in Bengali (his

family had been long domiciled in Bengal) and who had written a popular life of Shivaji in Bengali in which he first brought in the name of Swaraj, afterwards adopted by the Nationalists as their word for independence...He published a book entitled *Desher Katha* describing in exhaustive detail the British commercial and industrial exploitation of India. This book had an immense repercussion in Bengal, captured the mind of young Bengal and assisted more than anything else in the preparation of the Swadeshi movement.

The Mahratta of Pune, in its tribute to Swami Vivekananda (July 13, 1902), after his passing, spoke of how the Swami 'bitterly felt that India had completely degenerated; and [how] his idea of curing her was to make her recognise that in spiritualism lay her strength and what was wanted was only faith in herself... 'You have been told and taught that you can do nothing; and non-entities you are becoming every day,' it quoted Vivekananda.

In his opus, *Militant Nationalism in India: and its socio-religious background* (1897-1917), Biman Behari Majumdar observes that the 'triumphant return of Swami Vivekananda from his first Western tour in 1897, opened a new era in the history of nationalism in India. India had never before heard such a message of neo-Vedantism, strength and fearlessness and, above all, such a clarion call to abjure all the deities except the Motherland for the next fifty years...'

Swami Dayananda and Bankim Chandra Chattopadhyay's influence on revolutionary nationalists can hardly be minimised, as they paved the way for a renewed cultural quest. This in turn, drove the quest for political freedom, articulated most vocally and effectively by the latter. Bankim Chandra, writes historian Leonard Gordon, 'consciously channelled religious discussion in a political direction and helped bring about the fusion of religion and politics which so excited many young Hindu Bengalis and so disturbed officials early in the twentieth century.' Through his use of the Bengali medium, Gordon argues, Bankim wanted to, 'link the Western-educated few and the Bengali educated many through their common language.' Positions enunciated by these thinkers, reformers and masters led to the questioning of the then prevalent old political assumptions. Philosopher Ram Swarup wrote:

...old politics became outdated. The new spokesmen taught us to look at the country and its Independence struggle in a particular way. They taught that India was more than a geographical entity, that it was a holy land, a sacred trust, a spiritual idea, a power of the spirit, even a deity; they taught that India was rising for the truth it embodied, for recovering its *svabhava*.

This 'gave deeper ideation to the Independence struggle and a deeper definition of India.' Most of the revolutionaries who faced marginalisation, were inspired by and in tune with this dimension of our freedom struggle, which for them was not a mere political struggle but a more deep-rooted movement for the recovery, expression, and repositioning of the cultural self and all that defined and expressed it. Was it also because they spoke for such a self-expression, refused to reject the need for cultural freedom and recovery that their legacy faced marginalisation and their contributions were minimised?

With their legacies marginalised, their contributions minimised, their actions misinterpreted and their achievements negated, these personalities were cast aside, their heroic deeds and meditations for a free India forgotten and blanketed. On the occasion of the seventy-fifth anniversary of India's independence, such forgotten legacies need to be reinstated, given their due and made a vibrant part of the new and inclusive narrative of our freedom struggle.

The legacies of several revolutionary nationalists across India have suffered the same fate of forgetfulness or deliberate omission. Bengal is one such province where there has been purposeful apathy, especially over the last four-odd decades. Ironically, Bengal's legacy of revolutionary nationalism is one of the richest and most varied and yet it has faced both neglect and misinterpretation. The revolutionary legacy of Upendra Nath Banerjee (1879-1950), with whom we are concerned in this volume, who drew his inspiration from Swami Vivekananda and went on to actively engage in revolutionary work under the tutelage and leadership of Sri Aurobindo, has also been a victim of such apathy.

Upendra Nath Banerjee was a political thinker and a man of action, revolutionary associate of Sri Aurobindo, a principal accused in the historic Alipore Bomb Trial, a Cellular Jail deportee, prolific writer and a legendary editor. He was also a leading litterateur of his era. His Bengali memoir of life in the Cellular Jail entitled *Nirbasiter Atmakatha* (1921), became a classic and was the first such work in the genre of deportation and imprisonment memoirs to be written during the early 1920s in-spite of the possibilities of a clampdown from the colonial state machinery. Gurudev Rabindranath Tagore was so impressed with Upendra's style of Bengali writing that he expressed a wish to meet the writer and also encouraged his students in Visva Bharati at Santiniketan to read it.

Upendra is said to himself have translated his classic into English and it appeared at a later date and has been long out of print. In reissuing the English version of his opus, we hope to reach a wider audience to make them live through the ordeals faced by Upendra and his revolutionary colleagues, all political prisoners dumped and exiled, staring at death for having shown the temerity to wage a war against the 'Emperor' and the 'Empire.'

Around the time when Upendra and his colleagues began setting up their network of secret societies, launched *Jugantar*, began plotting insurrection in regiments of the British Indian army, planned to impart martial training to those who were joining the ranks of revolutionaries, the British Empire was in fact at its apogee. For instance, British historian Niall Ferguson in his *Doom: The Politics of Catastrophe* (2021), describes the extent and reach of the British Empire thus:

> ...In 1860, the territorial extent of the British Empire had been some 9.5 million square miles; by 1909 the total had risen to 12.7 million. It now covered around 22 percent of the world's land surface – making it three times the size of the French empire and ten times the size of the German – and controlled roughly the same proportion of the world's population: some 444 million people in all lived under some form of British rule. According to the St James's Gazette, the Queen Empress Victoria held sway over one continent, a hundred peninsulas, five hundred promontories, a thousand lakes, two thousand rivers, ten thousand islands...

Barin's and Upendra's bunch of revolutionaries, Sri Aurobindo himself and his band in *Bande Mataram*, Veer

Savarkar, who would have followed Upendra to '*Kala Pani*', the likes of Jatindra Nath Mukherjee, who planned an insurrection in the British Indian Army, the taking over of Fort William in Kolkata, and attained martyrdom in the 'Battle of Balasore', Rashbehari Bose, to name a few, had all challenged the Empire when it stood at its peak.

Those challenging its might have often been passed off as foolhardy and callow-minded upstarts who had no idea of the magnitude of what they were taking on. The reality was otherwise, the drive to achieve freedom, to form a free government of free India was so intense, dependence and exploitation rankled so much that most of these young boys gave up a life of comfort and often of plenty too, and joined the ranks of revolutionaries.

Their early political activism, their efforts to generate a political narrative and discourse on freedom, to give it an ideational contour and intellectual shape and to work it out on ground, in fact prepared the ground for later mass movements under Mahatma Gandhi's leadership. In his opus *The Intellectual Roots of India's Freedom* (1893-1918), Prithwindra Mukherjee focuses in great detail on this dimension of the freedom struggle. Mukherjee's thesis, completed at the Sorbonne under the supervision of some of the most well-known French political philosophers and historians of the modern era such as Raymond Aron (1905-1983) and Emmanuel Le Roy Ladurie (born 1929), focuses entirely on the early revolutionary nationalists who ignited and shaped the demand for India's freedom in the pre-Gandhian era.

The igniting of the aspiration of freedom, the pain of seeing India despoiled, the excruciating sense of wanting to uproot and overthrow the colonial dispensation, the hope of someday seeing

India being a leader in the world, of resuming the position of *'Viswa Guru'* drove these youth into the revolutionary struggle for India's independence. Mukherjee argued that 'Most Indian thinkers – beyond their nationalist dreams – maintained some humanitarian and international objectives, putting to practice the essence of a traditional wisdom that reminds constantly: *No one is a stranger to you.*' In the narrative of the freedom movement, these revolutionaries have often been given short-shrift by ideologically motivated chroniclers who have often in the past received official patronage to produce and promote their biased theories.

Veer Savarkar in his magnum opus *My Transportation for Life*, which has been read across generations and over decades quotes and refers to Bengal revolutionaries such as Ullaskar, Indubhushan, Nani Gopal, Upendra Nath, among others. Savarkar describes the hellish tortures, torments and abuses which political prisoners had to undergo in the Cellular Jail. 'If dacoits, robbers and other confirmed and dangerous criminals found it beyond their endurance to go through the hard labour, it is easy to imagine how the political prisoners must have felt...' He then cites a most poignant passage from Babu Upendra Nath Banerjee's memoir.

The passage is the one in which Upendra describes his extreme angst and helplessness with his palms skinned and raw and with blood trickling from the cracks in his hands, facing abuse because 'at the end of the day the yield [coconut oil which the prisoners had to produce by being chained to the oil press – the *Kolu* – and by turning it around] had not come to the regular quantity of 30lbs a day':

> ...I felt I was swooning; I heard abuses hurled at me by the petty officer in charge; I felt them like whips

against my heart, and, at last, I was dragged before the jailor. He abused me downright with the choicest slang and threatened me with caning. I was brought back... and seated in my place for the evening meal. Grief, pain and insult choked my throat and I could not swallow a morsel of the food put before me. A Hindu petty officer took pity upon me, and whispered to the cook to serve me more rice. He said, "The Babu is stricken with grief. He cannot eat his bread, give him some more rice." This made me cry aloud and burst into a loud wail. I tried to control myself and stop this exhibition. A blow with a stick would have been borne at that time better than these words of pity and compassion from the mouth of my fellow prisoner, the Hindu petty officer.

In the English version of his work also Upendra describes this episode (pp.119-120) and remembers being seized by 'a heart breaking sense of misery and rage.' The jails in the 'British Government', Upendra observed, 'do not reform character and in ninety-nine cases out of a hundred they drive a man furiously to the lowest depths of criminality. In our days at Port Blair the authorities had no ideas of reforming criminals. For them, the convicts were working machines and the competency of an officer was measured by the turn-out of these human machines under his particular supervision.'

Upendra's description of the vicissitudes of life in the Cellular Jail is both lucid, poignant, dipped in humour and yet, evokes a deep pathos that lingers with the reader long after the tome has been put aside. It is these dimensions which set apart the original Bengali in this genre of literature. Every chapter is replete with interesting details and minute observations, which make the narrative both vivid and hitting. Upendra describes the strange regulation of Brahmins having to 'give up their sacred threads' as soon as they entered the jail, 'such was a peculiar rule of the jail, though clearly, it was an interference with our religion.' Curiously enough, Upendra notes, 'nobody cared to meddle with the symbolic beard of the Mussalmans, or with the long hair of the Sikhs. It was the Brahmin who was the victim of this liberal spirit.'

His description of the 'Regulation food' is revulsion inducing and yet made with a tinge of satire, 'One can somehow or other manage with coarse Rangoon rice and equally coarse home baked bread', he recalled, 'but the most famished Bengalee youth would pause before a dish of arum, green and unpeeled plantains, and Indian spinach all boiled into a horrid mess along with gravel and rat's muck...' This was to be their staple for the next decade! Yet throughout his narration of life in exile in the Cellular Jail, Upendra kept himself and his role completely on the margins, opting to describe and focus on the intense hardships, deprivations and atrocities. He did not highlight himself nor did he glorify his role, nor did he try to attract the readers' compassion towards himself. Instead, in his inimitable style, he narrated a phase, events and episodes which were unheard of. This approach made Upendra's book an instant hit with the Bengali intelligentsia of that era.

A large corpus of such inspiring, thought-provoking, unnerving and elevating memoirs of different revolutionary genre was churned out and yet over the decades, especially after independence, they were lost in discourse and hardly any collective effort was made to retrieve or reprint these for larger dissemination. The narrative of India's freedom struggle saw a number of gate-keepers – ideological and political - who ensured that the narrative was monochromatic, one-sided and manipulated, and made to fit certain political and social theories of struggle and class conflict.

Personalities such as Upendra Nath, who displayed a remarkable intellectual calibre were besides being political activists also political theorists and ideologues, who stood their political ground, often going against the tide, who ceaselessly advocated the need for broad-basing the movement for it to be successful, who went on to oppose the communal politics of the Muslim League, opposed the creation of Pakistan, proposed and supported the movement for the partition of Bengal in 1947 and the creation of West Bengal, who laid the ideational ground for it, and through the power and popularity of their columns and editorials, mobilised public opinion in favour of this epic move. They collaborated closely with leaders such as Dr Syama Prasad Mookerjee, and joined the Hindu Mahasabha driven by their concern over the fate of the Hindus of Bengal, believing that they had been deliberately cast aside, enmeshed by the fences of silence and feigned ignorance.

Upendra Nath's was a many-sided life containing dramatic elements of revolution, spirituality and politics, along with incarceration, extreme torture, intense political activism, a prolific literary and intellectual quest, a constant engagement with the world of journalism, editorship and, in the final years, a decisive contribution to Bengal's political direction which integrated his name with the province's history.

As a twenty-seven-year-old, he set out to join the *'Jugantar'* group of revolutionaries then led by Barindra (Barin) Kumar Ghose (1880-1959), Sri Aurobindo's younger brother. A chance copy of the *'Bande Mataram'* edited by Sri Aurobindo fell into Upendra's hands, electrifying him to join the revolution. A master of satire and humour-laced rhetoric, Upendra's memoirs of life as an exile displayed his rare quality, hardly seen in other such works, of laughing at himself and of looking at the lighter side of events. His memoir does not get into details of the revolutionary work as it was written at a time when it risked being proscribed. It is often interspersed with wry humour and at the same time succeeds extremely well in describing life in that devilish jail. Despite enduring extreme hardship for over a decade, Upendra never lost his sense of humour. In his words:

All over Bengal things had already begun to hum. In the columns of the Sandhya, Upadhaya Brahmabandhav had been dressing out his *bon mots* in an appetising and peppery style; Arabindo Babu had come over to the National Council of Education after having chucked off his billet in the Baroda State; and Babu Bipin Chandra Pal had cut the old Congress party. For myself, I had just sloughed off my Sadhu's holy robes and was trying to fit myself into the strict clothes of the schoolmaster, when fate threw into my way a chance copy of the "Bande Mataram." In its leader, devoted to a speculative discussion about the political aspirations of India, the paper remarked: "We want absolute autonomy free from British control." Such an observation is now heard up and down the land on everybody's lips; but in those days even the big political bogeys could hardly muster courage to give it a voice... That bold comment of the "Bande Mataram" wormed up into my brains and fixed me up like a vice. A voice within my heart began to shriek out every now and then, "Arise! Awake! The hour will be just over."

It was a time when the revolution's early sparks had ignited as Nolini Kanta Gupta, Upendra's protégé in the early years of the freedom movement[4] described it, 'Calcutta was at the time in the throes of a great turmoil. The press and the platform were loud with cries of "Freedom" and "Boycott": the British must be driven out; India must be rid of the Britisher. In the parks and wherever there was an open spaces, crowds would gather to listen to lectures and orations, crowds mostly of boys from the schools and colleges...Swadeshi, boycott, national education, rural uplift – these were the slogans dwelt upon everywhere. And with it all there went on, in secret, underground preparations for revolution and armed attack.' Nolini Kanta writes, 'Almost overnight how very different we became from what we had been as individuals! We used to be just humdrum creatures, most ignorant and inert; now we became conscious and alert, our lives acquired a new meaning, an aim, a purpose...'

Upendra joined the ranks of the Jugantar revolutionaries in 1906 and his first revolutionary act ended with his return

---

4   Of his association with 'Upenda' [da is s respectful manner of addressing an elder brother or senior in Bengali], Nolini Kanta Gupta writes, 'Upenda occupied the position of both leader and teacher. It was he who taught us the Gita at the Maniktolla Gardens. Here in living in jail [in Alipore Jail as an under-trial in the Alipore Bomb Case]. By living in his company I learned a lot of things from him, he gave me much courage and energy and enthusiasm and some very good advice. I am grateful to him for all that...He had given me a suggestion as to what sort of defence I should put up in court. "You should say', he explained. "that you do not know anything, that you met me accidentally at your Mess, and that it was I who on finding in the course of our talk that you were interested in Indian philosophy invited you to come to my readings in the Gita's philosophy. You had no other motives or evil intentions." Upenda had also explained to me certain ways of doing meditation and this helped me pass some of my time in jail." It was largely due to Upendra that Nolini Kanta was acquitted and saved from being consigned to the dreaded 'Kala Pani.'

from the death-hole of the Cellular Jail in 1920. In between, surfaced a compelling urge to undertake *Sanyasa* and adopt the life of a *Parivrajaka* in the quest for a deeper national liberation. It saw Upendra travel across India, from the Himalayas to the banks of the sacred Narmada. During this period, Upendra spent two years at the 'Advaita Ashrama in Mayawati, where he practised Yoga and studied Vedanta.' His intention was also to seek from the sages and rishis the direction India's struggle for freedom should take. This experience internalised Bharat in him, inspired undoubtedly by the life and mission of Swami Vivekananda.

Born in Chandernagore, then French India, Upendra was attracted and deeply influenced by Swami Vivekananda in his early years and had the opportunity to hear the latter's address in Kolkata…Aged 16 or17, Upendra was galvanised into action by the Swami and the constant news of ill-treatment of his countrymen by their colonial masters. 'The daily news coming that in some of the streets and roads of my country Indians were prohibited from walking, the daily news of Indians being killed by heavily booted kicks of British officials and commoners alike, the daily news of '*feringhis*' molesting our mothers and sisters in trains, of missionaries penetrating the interiors of our country and breaking homes and families, of innocent tribals being transported as bonded labourers in tea gardens', deeply disturbed and unsettled a young Upendra and pushed him into nationalist action. Swami Vivekananda's sudden passing left him dejected and in despair, but he remembered having heard that before his passing the 'Hero' had promised that 'I shall distribute myself throughout the country'. This instilled hope in him and kept alive the revolutionary urge and aspiration to free India.

Upendra had also been in close contact with Motilal Roy (1883-1959), who had sheltered Sri Aurobindo in Chandernagore before his departure for Pondicherry. In later years, Roy also founded the *Prabartak Sangha* in Chandernagore, the area frequented by revolutionaries and where Roy's house was a *foyer* for charting out their plans. As a student of the Dupleix College in Chandernagore, Upendra had his first brush with the Swadeshi Movement. Among his friend from Chandernagore, was the valiant Kanailal Dutta (1888-1908) who shot dead the approver, Narendranath Goswami, in Alipore Jail and was later hanged by the British. It was perhaps from Kanai that Upendra first heard of the paper 'Jugantar' run by a group of revolutionaries including Barindra Ghose and Swami Vivekananda's younger brother, Bhupendra Nath Dutta (1880-1961).

Over the next few years, Upendra grew close to Barindra, who was looked upon as some sort of an ideologue of the group and being one of its chief writers, he was actively involved with the running of *Jugantar*. His unnamed editorial in this widely popular and fiercely nationalist Bengali paper assumed iconic popularity. Upendra also served under Sri Aurobindo as a sub-editor in *Bande Mataram*. Sri Aurobindo remarked that Upendra and fellow writer Devbrata Bose were 'masters of Bengali prose and it was their writings and Barin's [Barindra Kumar Ghose] that gained an unequalled popularity for the paper' [Jugantar/Yugantar].

Throughout his life Upendra expressed a deep reverence and admiration for Sri Aurobindo. On his release from the Cellular Jail, Upendra visited Pondicherry where the former leader lived in self-imposed exile and participated in a number of interactions with the Master. Around 1921, Upendra, Barindra and their revolutionary colleague Hrishikesh Kanjilal visited

Pondicherry where every evening Sri Aurobindo interacted with his disciples and former political colleagues. These sittings were discontinued from 1926 onwards when Sri Aurobindo withdrew into seclusion.

It is said that Upendra would try and draw him out on political issues. Kodandarama Rao, a disciple who lived with Sri Aurobindo in Pondicherry around that time, has left descriptions of those evening talks and mentions Upendra in his reminiscences. 'Both Upendra and Barindra', recalled Rao, 'were great humorists, talented journalists and story writers, and they did not like the Gandhian methods of approach to Swaraj, and wanted Sri Aurobindo to lead the country once again to attain freedom.' Rao notes that Upendra had the 'highest regard' for Sri Aurobindo, and he attended 'the evening sittings before the Master only to talk about politics and somehow convert Sri Aurobindo to his views and lead him into the political arena...'

Barindra Kumar Ghose had converted the Muraripukur Garden House in Maniktala, then on the outskirts of Calcutta into a centre for revolutionary nationalists. It was meant to serve as a training ground in revolutionary ideology, and in handling of arms and bomb-making to prepare the revolutionary cadres who would work through the network of secret societies to spread disaffection against the 'British Raj'. Here, Upendra imparted the message of the Bhagavad Gita, Upanishads and also took classes in politics and history. He retained the role of an elder with sage and pragmatic advice for the younger lot. He was "Upen-da" to many among this lot, who continued to keep their links active with him.

In the Alipore Bomb Case, Upendra was among the principal accused, among the ring-leaders. Bejoy Krishna Bose wrote about the Alipore Bomb Case, the 'first State Trial of any magnitude in India,' in his detailed account of the trial written a century ago, "because it was held at a time when discontent reached its highest point in Bengal and it concerned people who were gentlemen belonging to the best society, cultured, educated and highly intelligent. The novelty of the cult of the bomb and shooting and assassination of men of high position lent an additional interest to the trial which reached its highest pitch when articles from the *Sandhya* and *Jugantar*, couched in rich and powerful language and breathing intense hatred for foreigners and impassioned love of freedom from bondage, were put in and read in Court as evidence of proving conspiracy to wage war against the King."

On release from the Cellular Jail, Upendra continued his active and prolific association with political journalism and activism. He continued associating with political stalwarts of that era such as Deshbhandhu Chitta Ranjan (CR) Das in whose popular journal *'Narayan'*, Upendra's *'Nirbasiter Atmakatha'* was first serialised and popularised. Upendra wrote regularly for the Narayan, participated in the Gaya Congress held under Das's presidency in 1922 and also joined the Swaraj Party at his behest when Das formed it in 1923. He was soon enlisted into the 'inner circle' of the party. When Das undertook a tour of the major towns of East Bengal to popularise the Swaraj Party's objectives and ideology, Subhas insisted on Upendra joining them.

Upendra's columns were in great demand in a number of weeklies and dailies launched by a number of nationalists of his era such as *Bijoli, Atmashakti, Swadesh, Sankha and Forward* (under the direction of Netaji Subhash Chandra Bose). Upendra's reminiscences of a youthful Subhas as Das's political lieutenant in the Swaraj Party and his own close camaraderie with him during this period make for interesting reading. His description of Subhas's political will and tenacity and earnestness is a moving account of Subhas Chandra Bose's political initiation and evolution.

In a moving article on 'Subhas' that Upendra penned in the popular Bengali monthly '*Masik Basumati*', in January 1945, interestingly at a time when Subhas was at his political peak, leading the INA and waging war against the Empire, Upendra recalled those early days of his leadership:

> Never in my life did I see such a tireless worker. Laxity is almost a universal trait of the Bengalis. We are rather fond of taking our time in doing anything, we procrastinate. Subhas was entirely different. He had, what in English is called 'Bulldog tenacity.' He never gave up something in the middle and once a job was started by him, it was to be finished. A must for him. And hardship was no problem for him; he was ready to go without food, rest, sleep to finish the job. So he was also not ready to tolerate the laxity of others working with him and any sign of it in others made him mad, though he often did not express his anger outwardly; rather he used to suffer inwardly from suppressed anger and disappointment. Sometimes he even wept like a child. When everybody was ready to go to jail, Subhas was not permitted by Deshbandhu to go to jail. Subhas felt so 'piqued' that he burst into tears. Seeing this Deshbandhu laughingly named him 'our crying captain.'

Upendra remembered how while campaigning for the 1922 AICC session, when they were feverishly touring the country, 'packed in third-class railway compartments with little possibility of food and sleep, Subhas bore no trace of discomfort, irritation or of fatigue.'

Upendra's writings of 1920s and 1930s, a turbulent and rapidly evolving phase of the freedom struggle, come across as thought-provoking and arguing for the need for a freedom movement to reach the masses, of ameliorating their condition, especially of the labourers and peasants. Upendra also spoke of 'Swaraj of the Mind' preceding political Swaraj, freedom – *Swadhinata* for pursuing *Swadharma*, and was also better known for his writings and books such as *Unapanchasi, Pather Sandhane, Jater Birambana* – to name a few. He expressed a number of political and social views and also appealed for deeply infusing the mind to connect it with the *Bharatiya* ethos, i.e., trying to imagine a free India with the right balance of duties and rights.

One of Upendra's famous revolutionary colleagues Amarendra Nath Chattopadhyay (1880-1957) of Uttarpara, Hooghly, in a moving obituary recalled Upendra's exploits and contributions in creating an intellectual narrative of the freedom movement. To Amarendra, Upendra was his friend, philosopher and political guide who sustained and drove him during some of the trying days. Amarendra's memoir draws a vivid portrait of Upendra's politics, journalism, and his many sided personality. In it, one also discovers the various trends and currents of the era when the Swaraj party was founded, when the erstwhile revolutionaries on their release from long spells of incarcerations were regrouping and reorganising themselves under the Swaraj party and the Congress umbrella. It also provides a peep into the ideational climate of the manner in which literary and political stalwarts such as Sarat Chandra Chattopadhyay, CR Das, Subhas Chandra Bose and others engaged with Upendra and his new spell of activities.

Amarendra's account is replete with details on how Upendra

conducted the popular Bengali weekly *Atmasakti* of which he was the editor and Amarendra the background sustaining force. *Atmasakti* used to be printed from the Cherry Press, which soon became a vibrant rendezvous point with Subhas and Sarat Chattopadhya frequenting the place to discuss politics, literature, ideas and strategies. By then, Amarendra noticed that both Upendra and Subhas had already struck a deep and jovial camaraderie.

Atmasakti was founded because as Amarendra recalled, Upendra wanted a vehicle through which he could freely write on political, social and cultural issues for educating the public at large – *Loksiksa*. In a short time Atmasakti became popular. 'I facilitated his work,' wrote Amarendra, 'and kept no control over the weekly. I had no illusions, nor did Upendra, that the weekly would be a successful venture since the British did not let a weekly of this kind run for long. It soon met the fate of a number of other such papers run by revolutionaries.' Later, Upendra handed over *Atmasakti* to the 'Forward', the English daily run by CR Das.

Upendra's writings of this era also brings to light his deep conviction that social justice and equity could only widen the base of the struggle besides ensuring a lasting and sturdy foundation of freedom. He wrote in one of his popular columns:

> Those who are scared to sit with us in the same row then we have to lift them up onto our laps. Those whom we have relegated to the last row, labelling them as fallen and untouchables, whose touch we say make us impure, we have to touch them and become pure, we have to confer the right of being human on others and become human ourselves. It is the principal and first duty of the worshippers of freedom to cut the shackles

of others. If we are unable to fill the hearts of those who have been ignored and neglected for thousands of years, with hope, if we cannot radiate strength in their stiff and weak arms, if we cannot make them part of our own being through the power of love, then the fire of this national churn will only end up in smoke...

[Translated from Bengali]

Arrested again in September 1923, because of his writings and his continued association with the Bengal revolutionaries, Upendra was incarcerated in the Alipore Jail for three years and was released in 1926. He spent fourteen years of his life in British prisons, out of which ten years were spent inside the Cellular Jail in the Andamans.

Upendra's columns gained wide popularity and readership, making him a household name in Bengal and Bengali journalism in the 1920s and 40s. He was also part of the editorial team of the leading nationalist English daily *Amrita Bazar Patrika* which was founded in 1860 and ran till 1991. Upendra's experience in running the *Forward* made him equally conversant with English journalism.

Even during the last decade of his life 1940–1950, Upendra played an indefatigable role as a dynamic, provocative personality, and a fiercely nationalist editor of the *Dainik Basumati,* one of the leading Bengali dailies of that era. Founded in 1914 *Dainik Basumati* had acquired a cult-like following among Bengali readers throughout the period of the freedom movement. Upendra headed the daily at the time of partition and independence. It was in the pages of *Basumati* that he advocated the need for the partition of Bengal with the Hindu majority districts of the province remaining as a state within the Indian union. To Syama Prasad Mookerjee's political demand, Upendra proffered the intellectual and ideational basis and argument.

By now Upendra had joined the Hindu Mahasabha and became a prominent member of the vocal intelligentsia in Bengal that opposed the Muslim League's oppressive rule. Eventually, he was elected Chairman of the Bengal provincial Hindu Mahasabha. What pushed Upendra to cast his lot with the Hindu Mahasabha and join hands with Syama Prasad Mookerjee can be gauged from a statement issued by him and another Hindu Mahasabha leader BC Chatterjee in December 1939 on the 'Position of Hindus in Bengal' under a Muslim League government. The Hindu Mahasabha under Mookerjee charged the Muslim League government of pursuing a deliberate policy of advancing the interests of only Muslims and of curbing, checking and injuring 'in every vital respect, the interest and claims of the Hindu community'.

It pointed out how the government servants were being posted on 'communal grounds in specially selected areas' and how the 'rules of retirement and extensions of services [were] rigorously applied to Hindus while favoured Muslims [were] differently treated.' It spoke of an increase in the 'desecration of temples and defilement of images' in the last three years and of how 'the rights of Hindus were violated during immersion ceremonies in connection with Durga and Kali Pujas.' It demanded an enquiry into the 'abduction and seduction of Hindu women', it argued that the official figures were alarming, but that there were many more cases which 'were either not reported to the police or where the Police took no cognizance...'

Syama Prasad also spoke of the 'anti-Hindu propaganda' that was being carried by certain newspapers against whom no action had been taken and how Hindu newspapers were being targeted by the government, 'The recent statement issued by the ministry showing the extent of securities demanded from and warning administered to the press, discloses how Hindu newspapers have been the victims of a progressive policy of muzzling the press', his statement noted. Undoubtedly, Upendra, through his columns and writings, played a major role in highlighting these discriminations and inequities.

The last decade of Upendra's life was dramatic and which saw the passing of the Pakistan resolution, Subhas Bose's escape, the start of his epic journey to liberate India and the formation of a coalition ministry - Syama-Huq Ministry – in Bengal, the last attempt at side-lining the Muslim League. In this ministry, Syama Prasad became the Finance Minister of Bengal and eventually resigned in protest against British crackdown on revolutionaries during the Quit India Movement.

This period also saw the introduction of the Cripps Proposal, the launch of the Quit India Movement, a cyclone and tidal wave in Midnapore, the onset of a debilitating Bengal famine in which three million people perished, Jinnah's 'Direct Action', Noakhali, demand for partition, Syama Prasad's call for dividing Bengal and retaining the Hindu majority districts as an Indian state, the end of World War Two, the creation of West Bengal and the Independence of India.

Upendra's columns in the *Dainik Basumati*, if dug out, would certainly give an insight into his mind and thinking. His mind must have been a world intense with insight and deep prognosis on the direction a free India would or ought to take and also on his beloved Bengal.

While speaking of symbolism and the essence of the seventy-fifth anniversary of India's independence being celebrated in many places as *Azadi Ka Amrit Mahotsav*, Prime Minister Narendra Modi argued for a need to write about the forgotten or lesser known chapters, episodes, personalities and writings of the freedom movement. Young writers, researchers and historians have been encouraged to write about these marginalised personalities and episodes who have contributed decisively to the struggle for freedom, but whose memories and legacies have been allowed to recede once freedom was achieved. This is a unique and a vibrant way to revive, retrace, and commemorate that legacy of the freedom movement for posterity.

The renaming of Mount Harriet as Mount Manipur by the Union Home Minister Amit Shah in 2021 as a tribute to Manipuri Maharaja Kulachandra and other Manipuri heroes who served prison terms in the Andaman for waging war against the British; the renaming of Ross Island as *Netaji Subhas Chandra Bose Dweep*, of Neil Island as *Shaheed Dweep* and the Havelock Island as *Swaraj Dweep* by Prime Minister Modi in December 2018 while commemorating the seventy-fifth anniversary of Netaji's hoisting of the Indian flag in Andaman & Nicobar Islands are all part of this national effort to reinstate crucial episodes of our freedom struggle.

'Great and prosperous nations', wrote philosopher Ram Swarup, 'value their *tapasvins* and their intelligentsia, their generals and soldiers, their men of industry and trade, their artisans and workers...' A nation aspiring to be prosperous and great with a history of freedom struggle must also recall their fighters of freedom and commemorate them in myriad ways. Only then can freedom and aspirations of national greatness be based on a sound and permanent foundation.

In the light of Prime Minister Modi's appeal and initiative to rekindle the wide and multi-dimensional spirit of the freedom movement, the reissuing of Upendra Nath Banerjee's 'Memoirs of a Revolutionary' assumes significance and relevance. It is to preserve his legacy, to record his contribution and to pass on to future generations the story of those who fought for India's *Swaraj* so that she could pursue her *Swadharma* unimpeded.

For Upendra, it was only the pursuit that mattered. As he once wrote (in Bengali), 'We want to free India and with it we want to free every Indian in the realm of his mind, economically and politically...We want a freedom which accords every individual full scope for evolving into perfect human beings who cannot be battered into a petty existence...we want a freedom which will not develop an economic, social or political system that keeps our people dependent on and looking unto others, but rather a freedom which will offer them complete opportunity to express their *Swadharma*. To be free – *Swadheen* – and to follow *Swadharma* is the same thing.'

Kolkata
June 2023

Anirban Ganguly

Selected Sources/Suggested Reading

- Upendra Nath Bandyopadhyay, *Nirbasiter Atmakatha*, [Bengali], published by Hrishikesh Kanjilal, Kolkata, 1328 [1921-1922].
- Upendra Nath Bandyopadhyay, *Bharater Swadhinatar Sangrame – Adhyatmik Prerana* (Spiritual Inspiration to India's Freedom Movement), Kolkata: Sutradhar, 1428 (2021).
- Supriyo Bhattacharya edited, *Upendra Nath Bandyopadhyay – Rachana Sangraha* (Bengali) Kolkata: Sagnik Books, 2015.
- Sandip Bandyopadhyay, *Upendra Nath Bandyopadhya: Revolutionary's Portrait*, (Bengali) Kolkata: Sutradhar Publications, 2020.
- Barindra Kumar Ghose, *Tale of My Exile*, Puducherry: Sri Aurobindo Ashram Publication Department, 2012.
- Veer Savarkar, *My Transportation for Life*, (1927), Chandigarh: Abhishek Publications, (reprint) 2021.
- Prithwindra Mukherjee, *The Intellectual Roots of India's Struggle for Freedom (1893-1918)*, New Delhi: Manohar Publishers, 2017.
- Prithwindra Mukherjee, *Bagha Jatin: Life in Bengal and Death in Orissa (1879-1915)*, New Delhi: Manohar Publishers, 2016.
- Chanda Poddar, Mona Sarkar, Bob Zwicker edited, *Sri Aurobindo and the Freedom of India* (1995), Puducherry: Sri Aurobindo Ashram Publication Department, 2012.
- Haridas & Uma Mukherjee, *Swadeshi Andolon O Banglar Nabayug* (Bengali), (1961), Kolkata: Dey's Publishing, 2004.

- *Collected Works of Nolini Kanta Gupta*, Vol.2 Kolkata: Nolini Kanta Gupta Birth Centenary Celebrations Committee, 1989.
- *Collected Works of Nolini Kanta Gupta*, Vol. 7 Kolkata: Nolini Kanta Gupta Birth Centenary Celebrations Committee, 1989.
- Sankari Prasad Basu, *Vivekananda O Samakalin Bharatbarsha* [Vivekananda and Contemporary India], Vol. 6, Kolkata: Mondol Book House, 6th edition, 2012.
- Manoj Das, *Sri Aurobindo: Life and Times of the Mahayogi (the Pre-Pondicherry Phase)*, Puducherry: Sri Aurobindo International Centre of Education, 2020.
- Sri Aurobindo, *Autobiographical Notes and Other Writings of Historical Interest*, Puducherry: Sri Aurobindo Ashram, 2006.
- Sri Aurobindo, *Bande Mataram*, Puducherry: Sri Aurobindo Ashram, 5th imp, 1997.
- Bhupendranath Datta, *Swami Vivekananda: Patriot-Prophet: A Study*, Kolkata: Nababharat Publishers, 1954.
- Bejoy Krishna Bose, *The Alipore Bomb Trial*, Calcutta: Butterworth & Co., 1922.
- T Kodandarama Rao, *At the Feet of the Master – Reminiscences*, Puducherry: Sri Aurobindo Ashram, 2009.
- Lalit Kumar Chakravarty, *Biplabi Jatindranath*, [Beng] Kolkata: Bengal Publishers, (1354) [Beng era].
- Leonard Gordon, *Brothers against the Raj: A Biography of Indian Nationalists: Sarat & Subhas Chandra Bose*, New Delhi: Rupa & Co, 1990.
- Soumya Basu, compiled & edited, *Netaji, Upendranath O Anyanno Sahakarmibrindo*, Kolkata: Choyaa Publishers, 2022.
- Ram Swarup, *Hinduism & Monotheistic Religions*, New Delhi: Voice of India, 2009.
- Amarendranath Chattopadhyay, "Amader Upen", in Soumya

Basu, compiled & edited, *Netaji, Upendranath O Anyanno Sahakarmibrindo*, Kolkata: Choyaa Publishers, 2022.
- RC Majumdar, *History of the Freedom Movement in India*, Vol. 1, Kolkata: Firm KLM, 2nd revised edition, 1971, rpt, 1997.
- Leonard A Gordon, *Bengal: the Nationalist Movement: 1876-1940*, New Delhi: Manohar, 1979.

CHAPTER I

IT WAS the winter of the year One thousand Nine hundred and Six of the Christian era. All over Bengal, things had already begun to hum. In the columns of the Sandhya, Upadhaya Brahmabandhav had been dressing out his *bon mots* in an appetising and peppery style; Arabindo Babu [Sri Aurobindo] had come over to the National Council of Education after having chucked off his billet in the Baroda State; and Babu Bipin Chandra Pal had cut the old Congress party. For myself, I had just sloughed off my Sadhu's holy robes and was trying to fit myself into the strict clothes of the schoolmaster, when fate threw into my way a chance copy of the "Bande Mataram".

In its leader, devoted to a speculative discussion about the political aspirations of India, the paper had remarked; "We want absolute autonomy free from British control". Such an observation is now heard up and down the land on everybody's lips; but in those days even the big political bogeys could hardly muster courage enough to give it a voice. So those few words put in blazing print made my heart jump. Such candour was a rarity in an age when the champions of National politics would never call a spade a spade. Even when these great men happened to grow thundering eloquent over questions of "self-government", they always qualified their ideal with a prudent epithet "Colonial". By this they managed to bag the game without burning their powder; for the trick left the law inviolate and at the same time commanded clapping applause from a credulous audience.

But what a malicious star was blinking at me at that moment! That bold comment of the "Bande Mataram" wormed up into my brains and fixed me up like a vice. A voice within my heart began to shriek out every now and then, "Arise! Awake! The hour will be just over". I had a sleepless night; and turning over and over in my bed, I made up my mind to find out if there were a dram of truth at the bottom of those words. Could they be all empty rhetoric?

Yet when I looked about I stumbled on such wild yarns as made my flesh creep. I was told that an army 200,000 strong were then sharpening their long swords in some secret mountain cave against the day of action; that arms and all that were ready; and that the provinces of India were on the point of filing out in the most formidable battle array; and that it was only laggard Bengal that kept them waiting. But these might be all facts, I thought. For, who knew which way the land lay?

By that time the Yugantar had made its glorious debut and was having a roaring time of it. It was thick on the air that the office of the paper was a den of revolutionaries. Revolution! The very word made my blood sing in my veins to a romantic tune. The long procession of Revolution heroes from Robespierre down to the latest firebrand flashed across my mind. I became mighty curious about those precious souls who were to bring about a Revolution in India and who were, so to speak, to be the living images of the future Freedom of India. A keen desire to see they were like seized me. The bare idea that I would be sitting idly at my fireside while others were busy liberating India behind my back was too much for me.

Looking in at the Yugantar office, I found some four or five young men sitting on a piece of mattress and heavily busy in effecting the deliverance of India. The insufficiency of fighting outfit came as a damper on me; but that only for the passing moment. The young hopefuls soon supplied with long talk what they lacked by way of war equipment. I found them wonderfully unanimous about one thing, namely, that it was mighty little trouble to knock John Bull tumbling out of India, and that the "Yugantar" office would have to be removed in a short time to the Government House where there was better accommodation. All their big talk and small hints led me to suspect that there was something very big and momentous behind the veil—something almost as big as India.

A few more visits brought me into closer touch with the authorities of the paper. Yes, unquestionably they were all born Bohemians. There was Devabrata who later came to celebrity as Swami Pragnananda of the Ramkrishna Mission. He had graduated at the Calcutta University and been studying the law. But one morning he awoke to find India galloping hard towards Freedom, and at once left the King's Law to take care of itself and came to the steerage of the "Yugantar". Bhupen, a younger brother of Swami Vivekananda, was also on the editorial staff. Abinas was a sort of housekeeper in this home of eccentrics. He had to look after the management of the paper and the home. I could not get acquainted with Barindra at that time. He had been off to Deoghar to escape the fatal reach of malaria. But when later I saw him, his spare figure which was all bones with a bare cover of skin, his broad forehead, large eyes, and thick nose all impressed me with the idea that he is one of those whose strength of imagination and intensity of feeling would break down all barriers between the possible and the impossible. In his college life he found Mathematics getting on his nerves, and had to throw it over in a hurry; since then, he had tasted the varied glories of playing on the "sarang", writing verses, and running a teashop at Patna. He had found so much grace in God's eyes that though a rich man's son, he had managed to experience the pinch of poverty. At the time of this narrative, he was running the "Yungantar" with a confounding capital of Fifty Rupees. No wonder that when we met, he convinced me just in three words of the prospective freedom of India,—a thing that would come on in ten years' time, and was inevitable.

Such an easy opportunity for undoing the bondage of India was simply too precious to be thrown away. I returned home, shouldered my kit, and then went to be safely berthed in the office building of the "Yugantar". Then after a few days, Devabrata went over to the editing of "Navasakti", and Bhupen on an East Bengal tour. Barindra and I were the only men left to run the "Yugantar", and I suddenly discovered that I was somebody.

It was surely a new age for Bengal. All the young blood of the province was a-fire with delirious hopes. "Thousands of souls,—all strangers to fear, and all that had cried quits with the world!" A breath of Heaven must have roused the sleeping soul of Bengal, or was it a flood of light from some unknown region that swept the obscure corners of the heart where darkness had gathered for years and years? "Life and Death were like slaves at the feet, and hearts—they were free from all cares"—this pen-picture by Rabindranath was drawn from the life of young Bengal of those days. A new faith and a new optimism were brimming over in all hearts. We felt that we were the only imperishable truths, and that the Britisher with all his horrid guns and shells was just an illusion. Yes, we could blow down his ugly mighty house of cards with a single whiff of our breath! Our paper sang to this tune, and the echoes made our own hairs stand on their ends. We felt as if the soul of the country was speaking through us.

The "Yugantar" sold like hot cakes. One thousand— five thousand—ten—twenty thousand copies every week—that was how the sale leapt up in the course of a single year. The thing could scarcely be managed in one press; and we had to get it done secretly at other printing houses. But contrasted with this tremendous expanse, our business methods were quite hopeless. A broken box to put money in rested all the time in a corner of the office room. It was always unlocked. Nobody bothered about the incomes and the expenditures, for we were not out for money-making. From time to time a group of young souls came to stop at the office building, and had food and board there free of cost. None cared to enquire about where they hailed from or what they were. We only knew they were our compatriots! That was introduction enough.

Very often, as we went outdoors we stumbled on a man or two who seemed to stand watch over us. On our approach they would either be intently studying the heavens or be whisking off into the neighbouring tea-shop. Occasionally they would assume the innocent looks of a casual passer-by and move off whistling. We heard they were the myrmidons of the Criminal Investigation Department. But who the dickens cared a pin for C.I.D. or such silly stuff?

So passed our days in wild unconcern, till a circular came from the Government warning us against the seditious character of the "Yutgantar", and threatening us with the law if we would not take care to change our tone. But to us it came as a big pretentious fun, and made our sides burst with laughter. The Law! and that to come frowning on us! Not a bad idea of frightening us, thought we. But it must be a very comic sort of "Law" that would scare the would-be kings of this great India, the rightful successors to the Government House! We asked ourselves, "who may these blooming lords be to threaten us with the d—d law?"

But the Law, like the wolf in Aesop's Fable came all right at the fatal end. One day Mr. Purna Lahiri, Police Inspector, dropped in with a lot of "cops" and informed us of his wishes to search our office. He also showed us a warrant duly sealed for arresting the Editor of the "Yugantar". We were immensely delighted, but it was no easy job to clasp hold on the editor. Who was the man? Every one of us only too emphatically declared that he and he only was the person in question. At last Bhupen's [Bhupendranath Datta] bulky figure, and respectable-looking crop of beard got him netted. He more than others looked the man, and gloriously let himself be carried off. When the case came up for hearing in the Courts, Bhupen made no show of a defence. The whole of Bengal was shaken into a convulsion. It was a big surprise—a positive bolt from the blue. The Government sought to induce Bhupen to plead not guilty and be let off. But he was relentless and the result was that he was tried and sentenced to one year's R.I. by the Magistrate, Mr. Kingsford.

This was soon followed by an amazing rich crop of seditious cases. Within two weeks of Bhupen's sentence, the "Yugtantar" was again summoned before the Bench; and this time Basant Kumar, the Printer, was sent to his share of the grind. The process dragged on. Many a young man fell into the toils of the Law, and disappeared beyond the iron gates of the prison. At last Barindra said, "It is no use wasting strength like this. The Britisher can't be floored by big talk. We must make our theories see some practice."

This was the beginning of the Maniktola garden affair.

The Manicktola gardens were a piece of family property of Barindra. We decided to hand over the management of the "Yugantar" to a new batch of young men, and run a new venture at the gardens with only a select few. The terms of selection were at once laid down. These broadly demanded one specific qualification, namely, either a man should have nobody to bother about, or that having somebody to bother about he would not stoop to do it. In any case it was necessary that a member of this society must be ready to stride on to death at any blessed moment. But it occurred to some of us that this sort of sturdy mentality could only stand on a solid spiritual base. So a scheme of spiritual discipline was at once devised.

As an old recanting game, back from the line of the "Sadhus", I had little faith in any system of spiritual training that one finds in the books. But the "Sadhus" had always a fascination for Barindra, and spiritual training was his hobby. So the first thing he did was to declare his intention of hunting out a "Sadhu" who would help the spiritual upbuilding of the boys. Poor me! I had to keep him company. But there was no known spot on the face of the globe where a "Sadhu" might be lying in wait for us. Barindra spoke of a worthy living by the "Narmada", whom he had heard of in Baroda. This was certainly something to start with. Away we steamed off. But when we found our man, we saw he was not what we had looked for. That holy worthy could perform a hundred and odd astonishing feats. He could close up his wind-pipe with the tip of his tongue, and thus manage to suck nectar, as he said, dropping from the spiritual heights of the brain. He explained to us some fifty manners of uneasy, though unusually holy, postures of sitting; and he even got us to look on a lot of other equally rigid and hopeless performances. But we remained shamelessly unimpressed. So we bade him adieu after a couple of days spent in his college which, by the way, had entertained us quite regally.

This first shock of disappointment was enough for me. But Barindra did not appear to give in. He said to me "you just go to Giridhi. I have heard of a "Sadhu" about that place. You look him up. If possible, break your journey at Benares for a peep-in; I shall be looking about this side of the country for a little while yet".

I at once closed with the proposal, and with all the ostensible intention of travelling over to Giridhi, run up straight to Calcutta.

A few days later I heard Barindra had discovered another "Sadhu"—a precious one, who had fought with the Queen of Jhansi against the English in the Mutiny of 1857, and had since been vegetating in pious meditations in some sequestered spot. It was a dying flame which Barindra managed to set blazing forth. What the latter wanted of the "Sadhu" was only the robes of a "Sadhu" along with some mantras of any sort; for he said he could easily work out the rest. The "Sadhu" who had grown fond of his new chela in a short time, agreed, and had him initiated regularly. Many days afterwards, I happened to ask Barindra if he still remembered the "mantras". He replied, "Oh, that's clean gone off my mind." But at the date of this initiation, he had even an idea of setting up a sort of "Ashram" in the Central Provinces. Luckily the idea did not materialise, as the "Sadhu" shortly died of hydrophobia.

Barindra again hunted out a third "Sadhu" and got initiated a second time. This time it was a really great man whose spiritual powers were beyond question. I had the honour of seeing him later on, and was convinced of the extraordinary character of the man. However, Barindra came back after his second initiation and set our brains all running after the idea of an "Ashram". But it was so difficult to find out a suitable site. At last it was decided that pending the discovery of such a rare thing, the works of the Ashram would be carried on at the Manicktola garden.

CHAPTER II

AT MANICKTOLA we had a party of some five or six young men, and not even an equal number of shillings in all our pockets. All the boys were runaways from home, and were cut by their enraged parents. But they had to keep their body and soul together—a thing that to our apparent embarrassment meant money. So we got one or two of our friends to promise small monthly contributions which we proposed to supplement by gardening. The garden with its lot of mango and black berry trees held out a fair promise. This was deemed satisfactory as our meals were far from being costly. Rice, dal, and any sort of vegetable dish which could alternate with boiled potatoes—these were all we needed. If there was any occasion for hurrying, the rice and the dal could be cooked together into "Khicheri." The strict discipline of Barindra's sadhuism happily turned out to our economic advantage. Fish in any form, or onion was tabooed. Oil, pepper, and the like were also in the prohibition list. All this meant some paring off from the usual expenses of living.

Barindra's fertile brain soon discovered another new source of income, which was poultry-keeping. So a few ducks and hen were purchased. But it was not long before we found that the eggs had a mysterious way of disappearing, and the egg-layers unaccountably decreased in number from day to day. It might be either the jackals or the poachers, we thought. Then there were the neighbours whose religious sense was shocked by our keeping hens. One day a certain low class yokel boosed enough and read us a genuine orthodox lecture on Hinduism as as affected by 'hens'. This was certainly the last limit; and we could not help selling off our live stock. I have forgotten the name of that lecturing fellow or I would have sent his name to the Calcutta branch of the Brahman Sabha which would certainly be honoured by conferring some decorations on him.

But with all our laudable stoicism, we could not give up one luxury. It was tea,—the one item of useless expense. Absence of tea would take colour off our life, and force on the mind the grim truth of its mortality. This was more so, because Barindra excelled in the art of brewing tea. When we sipped that tea in the half-moon of a cocoanut-shell, our gratified eyes closed under a sense of appreciation, and we were confident that this precious liquid would be enough to sustain our enthusiasm till the declaration of India's freedom.

The first day of our "Ashram" life, Barindra ordered that we should prepare our own meals. The order apparently shocked one or two of us rather heavily for they slipped away. Yet it was not desirable to let in a cook—particularly when the funds were at a deplorably low-ebb. But the business was so new and troublesome. It had been always the mother at home and the hireling of a Brahmin cook at the messes who had done the cooking for me in the days gone by. Even when I had been a tramp, and sadhu, I had always begged meals cooked by others.

Yet there was no help now. So we made a compact whereby cooking would be done by two's the turns going round in a circle. This made me dabble in the rare secret of the culinary art. But though a Brahmin with supposed aptitude for the job, I never really managed to be much of an artist.

Utensils too were useless luxuries for us. An earthen plate and half a shell of a cocoanut for each were all we had. These were cleansed after each meal. We did our own washing. Only, those who had more cunning than others exploited the labour of the less clever.

As time went on, some twenty boys from different districts of Bengal came in. Of these! the young ones were engaged in studies and five or six fellows, rather grown-ups, had to do Ashram works. "Studies" meant exclusive discussion of the "shastras", politics, or history; and 'works' meant hatching Revolution. There were boys of all descriptions, educated or uneducated according to the University diplomas. But looking back, I now realise that they were all of them animated by something uncommon. It is my experience that the so-called wild and irregular boys have a lot more stuff in them than those who are labelled "regular and steady" by the school master. But in the scheme of our national activities, these venturesome lads are not allowed an inch of space. They get bored by their school lessons, and the University shuts its doors on them—an indignant hint of what the wise world would do to them. But when it is something which means life or death, ten to one, these wild hopeless boys would take the field long before the timid, calculating lot, earmarked for deputy-magistrates. The former clear so much where the latter stumble and possibly break their necks.

When the works of the Ashram were once on the go,

Devabrata and myself left Barindra to take care of the boys and set off once more on a hunt after a "suitable site for the Ashram". Devabrata was not at that time much interested in our activities and was getting fed up. But he longed to visit saints and sacred places. So we two started together.

The first town we touched at was Allahabad. We took up our quarters in a Dharmasala and stopped for a couple of days. We had meals on "Puris" bought at the market place, gadded about the haunts of "sadhus", and kept to our beds for the remainder of the day. One day a local friend of ours conducted us to "Jhusi", where we found along the riverside deep holes like what the jackals burrow in, and some sadhus in these holes. In one of these we came on an image of Rama all covered with vermillion spots and with four or five copper bits before it, while a sadhu covered with ashes was breathing hard in a fit of asthma, some paces off the image. We were told that these sadhus had a lot of underground cells to do their devotional exercises in. But our friends gave us such a hair-raising account of these exercises that it blunted the edge of even Devabrata's curiosity.

From Allahabad we trekked to the Vindyachala. There we put our things in a Dharmasala, and set out on our sadhu-hunting. We chanced on one living in a hut in the centre of a meadow. We paid our humble respects, and sat down at a respectful distance. But the holy man entertained us with a rich flood of spittle and rare philosophy. He never bothered about his food, as a milkman of the locality would give him milk and sago in exchange for the few copper coins which the visitors would offer the sadhu as tokens of respect.

Returning from that prodigious combination of spittle

and rare wisdom to our lodgings I we found a Sannyasini in possession of our blankets. She had the regular saffron-coloured robes of her order and a trident. Devabrata who was a Brahmachari and would not even share a seat with one of the fair sex, smelled danger. He had too big a bulk which he could not thrust into any hole whatsoever at that late hour of the day. So he looked her up and down and asked gingerly, "What brings you here, please?" The Sannyasini replied, "I like honest company, the company of sadhus". "Sadhus? Then you have no business here. You see we are gents. We have nice clothes on, gold-rimmed specs." But she would not yield and said, "Well, your dress does not matter. I am sure you are sadhus in disguise."

We argued hard to rub it into her that we were nothing of sadhus and had no disguises. But she held her ground till Devabrata gave it up in despair, and went out to spend the night under a tree. Next morning, we got abroad on our usual morning rambles. But when we came back we found the Sannyasini engaged in cooking rice and dal which she had got from somewhere. By ten o'clock, the meal was ready and she invited us to it. Money and women are undoubtedly very great obstacles in the life of a Brahmachari, but nowhere have the sensible Shastra- makers prohibited dishes cooked by a woman. So we had a hearty meal; and the Sannyasini partook of what remained over. The tender, affectionate heart of a daughter of Bengal beat under her saffron dress as strongly as ever,—and we found it.

Our next halting stage was Chitrakut. At the Railway station, swarms of 'Pandas' of all description fell on us. We could not convince them in our mixed Hindi of our motives, which never had been those of a pilgrim. But they were never ready to believe us. So we made haste to pass beyond their jurisdiction and take up quarters in a dilapidated temple on the riverside. But the obstinacy of these people was astonishing. Some of them kept up the siege. They plainly did not see how a man could visit a sacred place and yet be no pilgrim. After three or four hours of patient waiting, they tired of the game and went back showering curses on us. Only a small wag of some ten years still persisted in making a plaintive speech. With one hand on his shrunken stomach and another cutting the air about Devabrata's face, the little one said, "My dear sirs, God and His creation are one. If you feed me, you shall be doing a service to God." Devabrata burst out into a laughter when he heard of this close relation of Hunger to God, and said, "Look here, Kiddie, what you said just now is worth a thousand and not a penny less. But I don't happen to have so much about me. So take this pice here and make yourself scarce." The God in this small creature took the hint and the pice and melted away." The temple where we took up our abode was a long way off from the peopled localities. There was seldom a living visitor. Some monkeys had been the inhabitants of the place, and moved about among the trees. A mile or so off there was a monastary for Vaishnava sadhus, built at the cost of the Raja of Rewa. Two different sects of Vaishanava sadhus lived there, namely the Achari and the Vairagi. It was on rare occasions that a sadhu from the monastery would stray into the vicinity of the temple. We saw only one or two.

It was here that a marvel was in store for us. One day, a sadhu came on—a young man and a native of Gujrat. He was travelling in those parts at the request of his "guru". Heaven alone can say how he smelled our concern with politics. In the course of conversation he said to us, "You people fancy that the people in these parts don't know the drift of things. But there you are in the wrong. When the hour comes, you won't find them rotting in isolation". We patiently listened to it all without hazarding any remark, and waited to see what he was driving at. He continued, "Let me tell you one thing. If you believe it you will reckon it mighty important. If not, well, treat it as idle talk. You must know that God has to come again on this earth to re-establish the sacred Empire of Dharma. He has not yet revealed Himself; but the sages, the holy men are doing their best to hasten the date of His manifestation. That date is near at hand. Then only India shall see better days."

I asked him how he knew it. He replied, "Why, it was Hanumanji, our god, who has communicated this to me. I was doing my devotions to Him before now. For a long time, I met with no success, and in despair meant to commit suicide. At the eleventh hour, Hanumanji appeared before me, and told me that." Even now at such a remove of time I don't know if the whole thing was merely a fancy of the young sadhu or if it had any bit of truth at the core. In a short time, however, we took leave of him, and resolved to travel over to Amarkantak, which stands near the source of the Narmada. I do not clearly remember how we managed to reach the place. The name of the railway station at which we got down, and the roads we passed through have all slipped off my memory. The only event of importance that has yet stuck to it is our sojourn at the hospitable house of an Assamese gentleman. We had to cover long distances on foot, before we could reach our destination, the Vindhya ranges. These did not strike us agreeably. They had such bald looks. The peaky Himalayas have a ravishing splendour; but the Vindhyas have nothing of the sort. Amarkantak itself was belted by dense forests and had a big Dharmasala just in its centre, Sadhus of the Ramayat sect had a den there which was always fogged with ganja-smoke. A ruined temple stood at the spot whence the Narmada bubbled up from the ground. The place was strongly reminiscent of a past age of Buddhistic influence. A few struggling edifices looked like Burmese pagodas and contained the images of Buddha. In others the Buddha image had been replaced by that of Ram or Krishna. The forests were infested with tigers and every now and then a cow or a goat was missed from the neighbouring villages. Only when the victims were men, the sepoys of the Rewa state would fetch their hundred-years-old musty guns and do their duty by firing some blank shots. But the people have got used to the ravages of the wild animals. Before entering the forests, they would offer some sort of prayers to a tiger-god, and if that did not prevent the tigers from falling on them, they would blame Fate, and rest perfectly consoled. The same thing was done by the sadhus who, however, always travelled in large parties whenever they would perform their parikrama of the Narmada. This travelling round the river from its source to its mouth is a curious ceremony. It takes no less than some four years to tramp along one side of the river all the way from Amarkantak to Gujrat, and back again along the other side. Yet numbers of sadhus are doing it every year. I saw some women doing it too. They measured the entire distance by the length of their bodies. I do not presume to know what all these strenuous practices result in; but I am sure that even the smallest fraction of these women's faith and zeal could make men of us all.

We wandered about ten or twelve miles in the forests. Here and there lay a village or two that strongly reminded one of those chandal villages described in Sanskrit literature. The dogs of the villages gave us a good one mile chase. We ran along the river bank till we came to a place stained with fresh blood and marks of the tiger's claws. Had we but a glimpse of the future trip to the Andamans, surely we would not have moved a foot to evade the tiger.

The whole tract of the land did not offer a few yards of God's earth to set up an "Ashram" on. So we had to descend on the plains. As soon as we reached them, we found a letter from Barindra awaiting us. It directed us to speed back to Calcutta.

CHAPTER III

WE AT once packed up our things, which, by the way, consisted of a waterpot, a blanket and a stout travelling stick for each. Naturally! this did not take much of our time, and we started on. Back at Manicktala we found all in a tremendous hustle. There had been a lot of new recruits. Ullaskar was one of these and had a bit of interesting and distinguishing history of his own.

He had been a student of the Presidency College of Calcutta. One eventful day, Professor Russel of the same college chanced to insult the Bengalee students. Next time, Ullas went to the college with a worn out piece of slipper somewhere under his clothes, and flung it with some force at the back of Mr. Russel. Then he cleared out of the college in a satisfied frame of mind. His next venture was a course of study in some polytechnic school at Bombay. But when he came back to Calcutta on some pretext or other, he found the city in a state of excitement. This led him to enlist with us.

Yes, things were already at a highly exciting pitch. Mr. Kingsford, the Presidency Magistrate, was at that time methodically removing the Nationalist Press to the grim leisure of the Alipur Jail. People had got madly disturbed by the outrages done by the Police. The affair was singular, one-side, and almost everybody seemed to be saying, "This order of things must change. We must blow out the brains of some of these cursed blokes," Our Society quite agreed with the "Vox Populi". So we called a general conference which decided that the biggest head over the length and breadth of Bengal was that of Sir Andrew Fraser, and that it was a head that could very deservedly be dashed into splinters. But a head like that rose out of easy reach, for it was set on the shoulders of a Governor.

However, we tried dynamite for our purpose near Chandernagore. The explosive was placed on the railway lines for His Honour's train to get blown off. But it failed miserably, not even shaking the train. Only a big boom when the cartridges burst,—but that was not enough even to disturb the sleeping Governor. A few days later, another chance came on. His Honour was to journey down to Calcutta from Ranchi or some such place. We lay in wait at Naraingarh, a railway station in Midnapore. Our bomb expert advised a hole to be dug at a crossing of the lines, and put the bomb there with a slow fuse attached. With timely action, it could not be but a successful job. But His Honour had such a luck! On the memorable day, our expert had a shivering attack of fever and those who undertook the exploit were all raw. The result of this mischance was that the bomb exploded all right, but did nothing more than wrench off a few rails. The engine was slightly damaged and the Special had to change it at Kharagpore.

This event gave birth to a rumour about Russian Nihilists who might have migrated to India. One day a relation of mine, a 'Government officer, told me that the rumour had a very reliable basis, and that it was believed by the infallible authorities. I cannot say what would have done if he but knew that one of the said Nihilists was taking tea with him like the most innocent lamb. However, the Police fixed Rupees Five Thousand on the culprit. The reward was big enough to induce some arrests. A few railway coolies were reported to have owned up. They got five or ten years of transportation according to the varying degrees of their supposed responsibility for the crime. This event has now been a part of a past comedy. But later on when we saw respectable people interned on the mere strength of police reports which were eloquently and zealously championed by the entire range of the Executive, we could not but recollect the old Naraingarh affair, and smile even though our hearts might ache.

But by that time the C. I. D. people began to sniff at our scent. So we thought of disbanding some of the men of the Society. A small party consisting of Ullas, myself and three others left the gardens and went on a tour round the country. We got to Bankipore Via Gaya a, and overtook some Punjabi sadhus of the Udashi sect.

Sree Chand, the first born of Guru Nanak, had been the organiser of this sect. The members of this holy community had long hair, and ash-covered bodies. Ragged wisps of a blanket were clapped round their waists by bits of a brass chain. Wherever they chanced to stop, they raised a fog of ganja smoke. Their leader was quite a vicious smoker—and could not open his lips before he had full one hundred and eight hearty rounds of smoking at a stretch. They used tobacco also; but the sort they used was so strong that a few whiffs could easily set our brains whizzing in a dance. It was these excesses which possibly led Guru Govind to prohibit smoking altogether.

There were two very young sadhus of about twelve and sixteen years respectively. They were growing their hair into plaits, just as our fashionable young hopefuls hasten the first appearance of the moustache by oft-repeated shaves. I was curious about how these young boys had discovered the world as an unsubstantial vision at their time of life. A few questions elicited the truth that they had been poor people and that their parents had got them enrolled in this community so that they could have food enough.

The sadhus had their bath early in the morning, that is, they washed all their body; excepting the hair which was washed about once a week. The dressing up of the hair was a very delicate and complex affair. In fact that process of dressing it up in rings one upon another till it grew up into a perfect cone was almost a fine art! After the bath, the sadhus would kindle their sacred fire and begin covering the bodies with ashes. All this time, they would also chant hymns. At nine or ten o'clock it was hour for "Karah Prasad." This was a unique preparation and was something like a Punjabi edition of the well- known Bengali "Halua." Offerings of various kinds to all the known gods of the pantheon have I tasted in my life, but this 'Kara-prasad' stands unrivalled. Taste it, and you are convinced that it is the only reality in this unreal world. It is sure to fill the hardest heart with a softening sense of devotion. At noon, the course of meals included all the magnificent things that every honest Punjabi could enjoy. They were 'dal and 'Roti' well-turned in clarified butter (ghee). The nightly meals were repetitions of the mid-day course. No wonder that in a very short time we began to pick up flesh, and our bodies had a healthy bloom. Often we were sorely tempted by this life of heavenly contentment to stick to the sect through thick and thin, and give over the Manicktala activities with all their attendant discomforts of food. But my evil star was then blinking and blinking at me like a cyclopian eye!

The sadhus were bound for "Dhuni Saheb," a sacred place for them. It was somewhere in Nepal. We at once made up our minds to accompany them. But they vehemently objected to our saffron robes which they could not tolerate. To them their sectarian custom of using ashes was the best means of attaining holiness. We had had no idea of this or would have certainly exchanged the saffron; for the ashes. But what could be done at this stage? The problem was growing into a hard knot, when an old sadhu settled the controversial point with a little thinking. He said that a truce was possible between the saffron and the ashes if only we could be initiated into their sect. The solution was cheering, and we agreed in a right respectful spirit. Things were got ready for the ceremony of initiation. A sadhu mixed sugar with water in a big bowl and brought it on the scene. The Principal dipped his toe into it. Then he took it out an ordered us to drink up the mixture. We did it with a few mighty pulls. The old man then uttered some "mantras," and gave us each a slap on the back—thus completing the august ceremony. We paid our best respects to our new "guru" and set out after the "Karah Prasad." The party of the pilgrims was made up of some five Bengalees, and some forty of the Punjabi sadhus. We finished our railway journey, and entered the first stage of travelling on foot. It was then apparent that the affair was far from being comfortable. Some thirty or forty miles a day through the thick forests that flanked the "Kushi" were trying enough. My feet got sore, and swelled as if they had elephantiasis. But the sadhus knew no exhaustion. Day in, day out, they tramped on and were sound as a top.

At last we crossed the Terrai and altered a small town in Nepal. It was called Hanuman Nagar. The inhabitants were mostly Hindusthanis with only a handful Marwaris who did business there. But all the Government officials were Gurkhas. The narrow streets with their happy fringes of footpaths were neat and clean. We had always feared to find Nepal as a centre of rough barbarism; but found out our error. The idea that we trod the soil of a free Indian State put our minds in a gay flutter of excitement. We greeted the land from the depths of our hearts, kissed its earth and took in some deep droughts of free air. The place was really charming.

As we passed through the small villages we noticed thatched houses and they were much finer than those of Bengal. The entire scene was one of spotless loveliness, with no suggestion whatever of dirty ragged penury. The villagers had sincere reverence for the sadhus. One day of the journey, I had a bad attack fever and was compelled to lie down on a field My companion went into a village for some water; but he returned with a jug full of milk. How could an honest, good-fearing layman give mere water to a thirsty sadhu ? I heard by and by that the sadhus had great privileges in Nepal. When hungry, they could take food from any place whatsoever with impunity. The law allowed it.

We came to Dhuni Saheb after long day of travel. It had a girdle of Sal trees. The name of the place had a very peculiar history. One Baba Pritam Das, a great sadhu of the Udashi sect had in the past achieved spiritual *siddhi* [realization] on the spot. His "Dhuni" was still kept burning there and the name of the place is derived from this sacred fire. A lot of wild stories were current about this Pritam Das. It was said that once some disciples of the sadhu had asked for some mangoes, and that the sadhu exerted his miraculous powers to make the Sal trees yield the desired fruits. After all, perfection in ganja-smoking was no small thing! Three blessed days we spent at the Dhuni Saheb, and then we again made for the plains. It was Bankipore once more. Some friends of ours at Bankipore promised us a nice monastery at Rajgriha [Rajgir] if we would but stay. But Bengal was then attracting us with quite a magnetic force. We had no ease till we could start for our home. On our way down we got a newspaper which reported that somebody had sent a bullet through the Magistrate of Dacca. It took us no long time to understand which way the winds were blowing.

Reaching Manicktala we found Barin had gone off to attend the National Congress at Surat. The Midnapore Conference of a few weeks back had given us to understand that the Surat Congress would be a pretty warm affair. After two or three days Barin returned. He had talked with all the big political leaders, Moderates, Extremists, and Radicals, and the result of his talk he summed up in the exclamation, "Worthless rogues—every one of them!"

We eagerly asked him to be more explicit. He said, "Why, it is our worthy friends of the other provinces. They had been all ready while Bengal was lagging behind,—was it not what those precious friends all along told us? But that is all sham; there is absolutely no preparation. The leaders only play the boss from their arm-chairs. The young lot have some heart for serious business, but they can't do anything except at the back of the bosses. I could not help giving them a bit of my mind."

The news threw cold water on our enthusiasm. We had always heard of the Mahrattas as ready for immediate action; but that must have been a hoax. Barindra at last broke out, "Never mind, boys, if these d—d fools don't come on, we must shift for ourselves; Bengal shall give the start. In five years she will break out in guerrilla wars. So get about it, boys, and recruit new hands from this very moment."

A fresh period of activity began, and there was a steady flow of new recruits. But soon we had occasions for suspecting the nose of the Police about our ways. We tried to be precautious. There was an idea of distributing our strength in different detachments over the different localities of Calcutta. But where was the money for taking so many houses? The idea stood no earthly chance of a trial, especially when we were hard put to it to get the bare necessaries of life for our boys. At last, we managed to get a house near Baidyanath [Deoghar] and remove our bomb factory from Calcutta. The gardens were left to be only a harmless ashram. Ullas went to look after the factory while I remained with the boys. Barindra had always been a man of action, and God never suffered him to roost in a corner. So he went ceaseless rounds supervising the various centres.

A mishap at this stage made our hearts sink like lead. It was the death through bomb explosion of the best boy of our Society. He had something in him that made him a common object of affection, and his death depressed us beyond measure.

I had been to Baidyanath to see the poor fellow. But I could not bring myself to stay there after the misfortune. It was evident that the outlook was getting darker. Yet there was no help for it. The way must be walked out, even if it led directly through starvation, danger, and soul-crushing bereavements. Our choice was made and there was no shirking it now. So our activities apparently went on in full swing, but deep down in our hearts there was a horrid sense of losing strength. The way before us looked so dark! We were sending out so many brave young fellows to meet Death, but were we ourselves ready to face the grim spectre? Even if we were, our movements were a groping in the dark. I cannot say how Barin felt at the time. But, even he seemed to be anxiously looking into his heart in search of something on which he could confidently rely. It is likely that this torture of uncertainty led Barin to invite the sadhu who had initiated him the second time in Guzrat [Gujarat] to come over to Bengal. [The 'sadhu' was the Maharashtrian Yogi Vishnu Bhaskar Lele, whom Sri Aurobindo and Barin met in Baroda. Lele 'helped Sri Aurobindo' to have an important realisation in Yoga.]

In February 1908, the sadhu arrived at Manicktala. A few days stay fully revealed to him our ways and means. Then he said, "you go the wrong way, my boys. This business demands clean hearts; otherwise, it ends only in useless bloodshed. In such a crisis, the leaders must not be doing things blindly. Those only who can look into the future or have God's mandate can be allowed to take the lead. You must prepare yourselves for the work by Sadhana."

We looked at each other with blank faces. Mandateor Fiddlestick! The question was to rid the country of the British. What had God to do with it? We let the sadhu understand so much. But he was not moved, and remarked, "It is not for you all—this seeking of the mandate. Only the leaders need do it. They should know the way before they lead others into it. Bloodshed may not be always necessary for freedom." This struck us like a tale out of the "Arabian Nights".

We questioned with a wise-looking smile, "Fact?" The sadhu replied, "I tell you only what I know.

Freedom India will have, but not by these means. I have found this out after twenty long years of meditation. I may tell you that a time will come when all power will quietly pass into your hands. You will only have to arrange the administration. Some of you come with me, and practise *sadhana*; and if you don't find out the truth for yourselves you are at liberty to come back." This occasioned a lively debate among us. Barindra said, "Nonsense! I am not going to drop out. To free India without a drop of blood ! That's rather too big a dose to swallow." But I was rather affected by what the sadhu said and I had half a mind to try the thing. If it would only lift off the mists from the prospects before us ! It was so hard to apply the mind to any work whatsoever before I could come to terms with myself.

So I offered to follow the sadhu with one or two others. Before taking leave of the Society he once more sought to persuade Barin. But the latter had never been in the habit of taking counsel. Failing to convince Barindra, the sadhu said, "But if you don't change your line, you would soon get into a tight corner."

Barindra waved his hands and said, "That means they shall send me dancing to the gibbet? Well, I am ready against all contingencies."

The sadhu shook his head and said "Worse than that and a lot more dreadful.' There was no more talk.

The sadhu fixed the day of his departure, I had thought

of accompanying him, but as the day approached, I found it hard to leave the spot. It had been no severe heart-burning to give up my home, my wife and son; and the thing had not cost me many a thought. But it seemed cruel to leave the boys to their fate. Had they not all run away from the tender comforts of their homes and thrown away all their promising futures to follow our lead? Then, there were the gardens which were closely associated with so many hopes and ambitious projects, so much love and zeal.

How could I leave them all—so many young souls ready to face death at our bidding, and so much of work already done? The idea cut me up like a rapier. I began to love my project of following the Sadhu less and less. And on the appointed day in March, we failed to accompany the sadhu who went away with a heavy heart.

CHAPTER IV

WHEN THE sadhu had gone back, we once again lashed up our jaded minds with brisk activity. It had been our original design to create a number of centres all over Bengal and organise our strength before breaking out into open revolt. But this involved not only patience and perseverance, but also time. It requires some actual experience to feel the difficulty of silently bearing with all sorts of shame, insult or torture for the sake of a remote ideal. Bengal had no patience, and what she wanted must be near to her hands. Her blood was up against the Government. So process of organisation was a distinct obstacle race.

Finances were another problem. The scale of operations increased, and recruits came on steadily, but there was no money at the back of the thing. The only means of floating the organisation from financial quicksands was to rouse the interest of some monied blokes. But these fellows demanded in, exchange nothing less than the head of a governor or the like. To reduce travelling expenses, the factory at Deoghar was again shifted to Calcutta. A house was taken at Bhawanipur [southern part of Calcutta] to accommodate the old members, while the gardens were at the disposal of the young recruits.

This was done to cover our tracks. But all our efforts could not throw the Police off our trail. Numbers of occasions for suspecting their motives were found. Persons of curious description began to stalk about the gardens. One or two men always shadowed us in the streets. One day as I was walking through the streets, I chanced to look back, and what did I see but a pair of big blazing eyes staring at me from over a big moustache? I turned many a corner and threaded many a street; but the eyes would not be shaken off. At last I got myself lost in the thick of a big crowd, and it was only then that I managed to move out of the fire of those baleful eyes. A month slipped by. Then came about that bomb- affair at Muzaffarpur. It was the death-knell of our Society.

A day, yes, it is a day that has stuck to my memory like a burr. April? Yes, it was April, then, and that grilling hot. All the long long day we had tramped up and down and returned to the gardens at evening. Weary, hungry, tired only within a few inches of death, I would not have run away to save my life even if it came to that. Others were knocked up to the same tune. But still hunger must be satisfied, and as I have told we were our own cooks. So the younger lot began to do the cooking, while we, the big older fellow, stretched ourselves and let our imagination loose into the rosy mists of future. But Fate overtook us. The pot in which the rice was boiling cracked and the contents were scattered about. The boys broke out in a roar of laughter. I saw the hand of Fate clearly, and crushing my hunger took the bed. But Barindra had an energy that never flagged. As there was no fuel he burnt newspaper and made a fire to boil the rice once again. At about eleven o'clock, a friend of ours dropped in to say that the Police had been thinking of honouring us with a visit and that we should shift the venue. It was a fair warning; but nobody seemed disposed to move out unless he was dragged off by the legs. So it was decided that each would clear off the first thing on the following morning. Yet Barindra took a party of boys and buried in the earth the few rifles and bombs that lay about. The clock showed twelve when we finally retired to our beds.

It might be four o'clock towards daybreak. Heat and mosquitoes had made a hell of a night for me, and I was tossing about on the bed in all restlessness when the sound of footfalls on the stairs came to my ears. A few minutes, and then there was a sharp knock on the door. Barindra started up and opened the doors to be questioned by an unknown English voice, "Your name?" Barin gave his name. The mighty visitor blurted out his orders, "Here, you, get hold of this chap."

Evidently the first chapter of the history of Indian Independence was closed at that point. But hope can die only with the spark of life. The Police were arresting all they could lay hands on in the room that was still dark. "Now or Never" thought I, and stole out at the other door into the adjoining verandah. The gardens teemed with the Police force, and I saw a perfect forest of red turbans. The thought of a broken window in the kitchen room flashed across my mind like a lightning. It was possible to jump out of that into the streets. I at once bolted it; but when I looked out of it, lo! the enemy was there in his grim superciliousness. Fate is certainly a whole-hogger; she allows no ways of escape when she closes on a man. Disappointed, I stole back into the verandah, and thence into a small lumber room leading away from it. The room was full of useless, broken timber and had been a secure home of rats and cockroaches. At a window, a piece of worn out gunny hung like a screen. I concealed myself behind it and watched the movements of the enemy through a number of chinks, the night seemed to be as long as Eternity. But at last the crows cawed and one or two nightingales might have also burst into ridiculous frolic of a song. The sky greyed in the east, and the faint light of daybreak revealed to me the entire gardens as one red patch. The coloured turbans of the Police were seen everywhere, in every blessed hook and corner. Some European sergeants were bustling about with big whips in their hands and some coachmen of the neighbourhood called in as witnesses to the search, were following with unspeakable humility at the heels of a gigantic person who might be an Inspector. Our men were seated by twos, under a big mango tree by the side of the tank. They had been all handcuffed; and Ullaskar seemed to be solving some academical problem which, as I knew later on, was the exact weight of flesh the gigantic Inspector was carrying about.

The morning wore on. Five, six, seven,— the clock gave the strokes and indicated the tediously crippling gait of time. I kept my post behind the screen like an Indian lady of the harem, and was hoping that the enemy would overlook me. But hopes are like reeds against the decree of fate. The huge bulk of the Inspector marched up the verandah and burst the doors open. It was such a tense moment. I squeezed my nose to stop breathing which might have a sound. But what a long nose the police have been blessed with! The Inspector came on straight to where I stood and brusquely drew aside the screen that had yet saved me from dishonourable violence. Then eyes met eyes, and there were sweet exchanges of amorous glances!

What a love shone in the light of those two pairs of eyes ! The Inspect gave out an ecstatic "hurrah"! like a second Alexander triumphing over a new glorious conquest. Four of his men at once rushed in and carried me to the spot where the boys had been sitting. A man came on to put handcuff on me at the bidding of the Inspector, and I looked up to the face of the man. True as wax I found in him the ex-bearer of our "Bande Mataram" office, who had served me tea many a time. He cast down his eyes as he put the handcuffs.

Meanwhile the search had dug up the bombs and rifles buried overnight. The police began to torture the boys for fresh information and more secrets. This was too much for Barindra who brought the matter to the notice of the Inspector-General, Mr. Plowden. The latter laughed and remarked, "You must not expect too much from us."

We were in the lock-ups at different police stations that day, and had no more luck that a few slices of bread for food. The following day, we were hauled up into the C. I. D. office where we were told of three more searches other places and of a lot of unjust arrests of quite harmless people. Ramsadaya, the Deputy Superintendent treated us with quite grandmotherly love. He brought forth an amulet almost as big as a drum, and told us that he came of the illustrious line of Kamalakanta, the great holy man, and that the amulet contained the sacred dust of that holy man's feet. It could, he continued, be a charm against all dangers. Then, he wept a good deal, and laughed much more as he sought to convince us of the fact that he had awful sympathies for us and our works. Were it not to save a family or a wife and a number of helpless children from starvation, he would have never been a slave in his official role, and wickedly run us down. Or, who would be a willing instrument of inhuman torture of a tyrant government? Another Inspector hailing from Baghbazar also shed a flood of crocodile tears and faltered out something which might be groans of penitence for his sin of arresting us. All this was, as we saw later on, mere blandishments to have us on and play us into a confession. But at that time, we had scarcely any idea of the shifting ways of the law, and so, soon fell into the trap. Ullaskar observed that we should own up if that would save the innocent. Poor fellow he reckoned the police were the incarnations of justice or sincerity of purpose. Barin said, "It is close-up with us now. But the public should know what we meant to do." This discussion about the propriety of committing ourselves was cut short by the bustling entrance of Ramsaday; with a scrap of paper. This he held out before our eyes and said with much seeming joy. "Look here, my boys, Hemchandra has filed a statement." I need not add that the thing was a blasting fabrication, and the blackest lie. But we were so much upset that we had scarce wits enough to look behind this falsehood. So in an access of regretful sentimentalism, we confessed our responsibility for one or two incidents. That sufficed or was considered to suffice for the day, and we were left undisturbed for the night.

By the noon of the following day, we were produced before the magistrate in the Police Courts of Lall Bazar. The excitement of arrests had subsided to a considerable degree. The boys all showed long wan faces. One of them said to us, "I am awfully hungry and can't bear it. They gave me almost nothing to eat yesterday. Only a few handfuls of fried rice,—what do you call it but starvation?" Barindra flared up and exclaimed out to Mr. Benode Gupta, an Inspector, "Well sir, you had better hang us as early as you can. But why the hell do you starve these kids?" Mr. Gupta at once ordered a Sub-Inspector to fetch any sort of food, and the latter deputed a Head Constable who in his turn passed on the orders to an ordinary constable. The outcome of this kindly fuss was that only a glass of water reached us after persistent demands. When the matter was brought to the notice of Mr. Gupta he frowned on and cursed a fictitious constable, and mysteriously vanished from the scene. After the Police Court formalities, we were driven up to the magistrate's Court at Alipur. On the way, the officers did us some service, which it would be an untruth to deny. They gave us some sweets from a road-side confectionary. At the Court they even *gave* some of us a few glasses of water so that we would not find our tongues parched when making the statements. But the last, only when the magistrate had rather sharply ordered the officer to do it.

There we saw Mr. Birley, the magistrate sitting high in his chair and looking on with grim face which was like a finished slab of marble. He looked every inch an embodiment of the machinery of the Government itself. He noted down our statements, and asked, "You think you can govern India?"

The question made us laugh in spite of our heavy hearts. We replied, "My dear Sir, were you here to govern India a century or so back?" Or, did we go to you for a few Governors?"

Apparently he did not relish the reply, for he ordered the reporters not to publish that bit of conversation.

It was close on the evening when the Black Maria drove us to the Alipur jail. The gates had been already locked, and there was no arrangement for food. But the Jailor found us some boiled rice and a quantity of dal. The things tasted like veritable ambrosia after nearly two days of starvation.

CHAPTER V

THAT NIGHT was no time for any sober thinking whatsoever. Barin had said at the hour of arrest, "My mission is over". But the words had not found an echo in me. Why, there remained yet so much to do for the country—for the dear Motherland ! Only we had come to the end of our short roles. All our burning ambitions, all the fine visions we had conjured up of a new age that we were to inaugurate, were cruelly dashed to the ground. The past burst out into a thousand pretty stars in the darkness of the mind. I recollected how one day I had come back home, tired and worn out by some four months of pottering about and how my mother had looked at me and said in a loving pique, "My own child has gone out of love with his mother and her home ! Why, my darling, are you a waif of the streets that you tramp about like one? You belong to a respectable family, but I am afraid the Police would insult you one day with arrest." Her words came about too true. Then I came to remember the remarks of the Constable who had whispered to me on the way," "Why didn't you fire blank, sir? Had you done it that would have been mighty good excuse for us all to scud." Fact. We were just driven into the jail like a flock of sheep. Even death could not make amends for one moment of that inaptitude. A sergeant had said mockingly : "They are such good lads. They didn't think it worth their while to keep an eye on the approaches to the garden. They went to sleep like the Innocents." The joke came now home to the heart with a bitter sting. Yet there was no remedy now. We could only gnash our teeth in rage and repent the lost opportunities. Once I grew mighty angry with Ullas. The fellow had been awake enough when the Police entered the gardens. He could have slipped away if he pleased. But the fool had stood as a dumb witness to the whole thing like the imperturbable Brahman of the Upanishads! The idea of escape had not occurred to him.

The night passed away through these painful regrets. Next morning, I got up for a peep out. Why, the pandemonium was full. All the boys of the different centres—the large crowd of political dissenters—were doomed. Even a few unknown faces caught mine eyes. Where the misery did they hail from? I asked one of them, "Who are you, my dear fellow". He whined out, "I live at Manicktala, sir. I went out for a morning walk into the neighbourhood of your gardens, but the Police got hold of me. I had no idea that morning walks could bring one within the limits of the Penal Code." Then I saw Nagen Gupta and Dharani, his brother. Poor fellows! they didn't even know what blessed thing a bomb was like. It was Ullas who suspecting the meddlesome snout of the Police had his bombs packed in a steel trunk and deposited it in the house of his friend Nagen. But neither Nagen nor Dharani knew what the contents had been. Ullas made a clean breast of the entire affair only to save these fellows. He had yet an idea that the police would not proceed with the case against these brothers after that. He did not yet know that the Police did not have the blood of the great truth-loving king Yudhisthir in their strong veins, nor have any strong penchant for truth and justice.

Gradually all the districts of Bengal came under the sweep, and many were those who got hooked. Sushil Sen from Chittagong, with his Brothers Biren and Hem whom I did not know; Krishnajivan from Maldaha, Biren Ghose from Jessore, and Sudhir from Khulna—all were penned in due course.

Then arrived my old chum Pandit Hrishikesha [Kanjilal] like a moving Colossus. We had been college friends, and our friendship had a history that will bear narration. We were class-fellows in the Duff College. Then when I severed my connections with the English learning at the College and was about to renounce the world as a sadhu, the Pandit had a rush of feelings and swore on the sacred waters of the Ganges at the Nimtalla Ghat that he would be sure to follow me on all honest ventures. Well, the Nimtalla Ghat, as everybody knows, is no less than a holy place; and the Ganges is as much of a conscious Divinity as one can imagine. So, there could be no going back on the promises made before such august witnesses. I do not know how the goddess—the Ganges— sealed her signature to the compact, but the Pandit has always been at my back. There is a distich in Sanskrit which defines the tests of true friendship. A real friend should follow his man to all places and conditions through festivities, calamities, famines, revolutions, the King's courts, and lastly the cremation ground. The Pandit invited me to the festive occasions of his wedding and of his child first taking the boiled rice. We both nursed the sick in the days of a famine and went out as sadhus shoulder to shoulder.

We were school teachers too at the same time. In the days of this tale we were in the clutches of the law and waiting to be tried as the members of a revolutionary society. We did not know at that time that future would find us in double harness in the Andamans. So, he has successfully stood all the tests devised by the Shastras with only one single exception, namely, the cremation ground. I shall be much thankful to go through that final clause of the compact at the self-same Nimtalla Ghat where it was first covenanted. But that is yet to come.

The Pandit had nothing to do with the Manicktalla affairs, and he knew very little of our movements. The Police screwed him simply because his name had been found once or twice in the papers of our Society. But the covenant acted like a piece of inevitability. Fate had already booked him for the Andamans along with me. When he had been hauled up before the magistrate, the latter concluded from his innocent, Pandit-like looks that the accused might be "not guilty". But my friend had again a rush of feelings, and lost his easy temper. I do not much relish the idea of getting into hot waters once again by quoting at length all of what my honourable friend spoke to the magistrate in criticism of the grand system of the British Government in India. But he dwelt or all interesting topics beginning with the tom-foolery of Mr. Fuller and ending with blooming compliments on the Viceroy and Lord Morley. The speech made the magistrate order him to be locked up in a solitary cell where he might revise his political views.

Before a week was out, came Devabrata. He had run the "Nava-Sakti" for about a year after his severance from the "Yugantar", and with "Nava-Sakti" drying up, had been engage in his pious exercises. But that did not help him to avoid the

Police. They clapped the irons on him, and led him into the jail. The same day, Narendra of the Sreerampore Gossain family, was arrested and closed in the fold.

The progress of arrests was not without its humour. In a note book belonging to our Society was a name "Charu Chandra Ray Choudhury". Indubhusan of Khulna was daubed with that name by us. But the omniscient Police hunted for the "Charu Chandra" and after a lot of plausible intelligence work they hit on Mr. Charu Chandra Ray, Professor of Dupleix College, Chandernagore, and landed him on the spot. The unlucky Professor had unconsciously committed a crime. He had been the Professor of both Kanai Dutt and myself, and had lived in the same Chandernagore with us. And according to the logic of C. I. D. the Professor cannot but be a criminal when two of his pupils were blatant revolutionaries. In the eye of the law, "Ray" and "Roy Choudhuri" made no difference. So in a few day's time some thirty or forty men were bagged and kept in the Alipur Jail. The distribution of this number was no easy thing. In three or four cells they put groups of three; and the rest were locked up each in a solitary cell.

The high tide and tumult of arrests subsided in a week and left us a spell to look about ourselves. I found myself along with two others in a cell some seven feet long and six feet broad. My companions- in-irons were young enough. Nalini Kanta Gupta, a B. A. student of the Presidency College aged about twenty, and Sachindra Nath Sen, a stripling of not more than fifteen. The former was as meek as a lamb. At a corner of this cell were placed two tubs that answered the purposes of the lavatory for all three. This was a bit rough on us ; for when one of us was busy there, the two others had no help but to close the eyes. A small fraction of a verandah projected beyond the cell, and there we could bathe and have our meals. The verandah looked over a poor strip of a yard, and beyond this yard rose the high walls of the prison. Our eyes seemed to be burnt with live coal, whenever we looked at these walls, which always seemed to be frowning and saying, "You are all prisoners, yes, prisoners. There is no escape out of this place after you once come within my reach." One could catch a sight of some portions of the blue skies and of the tops of an ancient Banian tree over the walls. That was all the poetry the prison life could boast of. Everything else was as much grating and devastating as the worst bit of prose.

But the most horrid thing was the Regulation meals. The first day they amused us; the second day they threw us into a blazing passion; and the third day they drew tears from our eyes. The breakfast came to us the first morning after our arrival to shock us. As soon I as we were out of the beds, a black burly fellow came in with a tub, and with uncommon gravity poured out a quantity of a white something into our iron plates. This was called "Lapsi" in the savoury language of Alipur. But what unearthly thing this 'Lapsi' could be? It puzzled us. Sachin examined it from a distance, and said, "I see. It is boiled rice, water, starch, and all these mixed up." Next day when it was served it looked yellowish, possibly due to its mixture with dal; and on the third day it was red. They said it was a royal dish of the jail population, because it happened to be punched with a bit of molasses.

At ten o' clock, a course of boiled rice of the Rangoon sort, dal, and a pot-pourri of leaves and stumps of tamarind was an unnecessary addition. The same course was maintained for the supper. The extreme repulsive character of the Regulation diet induced us to launch out into a discourse on the various points of healthy dieting when the doctor and the jailor came on. The medical man was Irish, and a gentleman at bottom. He patiently listened to our complaints, and said, "I can't help it. The Regulations are responsible for this. Only in case of the sick, I can do something. Otherwise I have no blessed right to interfere."! But the jailor said, "Strange! You must be having jolly good things. We have potatoes, onions, and a lot of dainty vegetables in the jail gardens." Sachin, who was rather sharp-tongued said to the jailor, "Yes, sir. You certainly have a lot of delicate vegetables in your sacred gardens. But they don't find their way hereto. Somebody must be meddling with the usual supply; or how do they pass off to other quarters? We always get the riff-raffs." But there was no change yet. So, the only means of life was to feign illness. We tried the entire list of possible diseases. Then we worked our brains for discovering any new disease that might not have visible symptoms. One was almost imperatively necessary for us—or there was no chance of life. One day Pandit Hrishikesh told the doctor that his left eye-lids had been all quivering for the past two days, and that he felt dangerously ill. There was no cure but the hospital diet. The doctor laughed and allowed his patient the option of a medicine.

But 'necessity is the mother of invention', as the imperfect proverb goes. We struck out a new way of getting eatable stuff. It was the influence of money. We soon came to know that if one could slip a few coins into the hands of the guards and the cooks, he could easily get fish and other like dainties. Money often worked miracles. It made the red turban of the constable produce cigarettes. And it very effectively answered another test. We had no sufferance to converse with one another from different cells. For a few days, we tried to snatch a bit of talk; but the warders began to object and threatened with reporting it to the authorities. But once we found to our surprise that they looked amiable and could not hear us though we shouted to one another. It transpired later that a friend of ours had choked their ear-holes with circular bits of silver coinage. Thenceforth, it was they who kindly warned us against the approach of the jailor or the Superintendent. What miracles gold and silver could do!

We had yet one trouble which seemed to be endless annoyance. This was the recurring visits with which the C. I. D. officers honoured us. They always spoke to a tune which was calculated to worm into our confidence. When we heard them talk, we were led to believe them to be our best friends, and really beaming with sympathy for us. Their bland manners could very easily ensnare us, had we not already been sufficiently familiar through our experience of one day. They had not visited many times, before Narendra showed a spasm of curiosity. He suddenly became interested in the history of our Society with all its different branches and their leaders. To this was added some very suspicious hints dropped by the authorities and all this clearly showed that something had gone wrong.

One day, Hrishikesh came to me and said, "Coin me some Madras! and Maharatthi names."

I asked him, "Why?" He replied, "Bet Naren is going to fake. Soon he will be an approver. Why not get some unusual names of fictitious beings, and let the whole pack of sleuths run after them? It will be capital fun."

I gave him some names. So a Purusottam Natekar became the Chief at the Mahratta centre; in Guzrat, it was a Kissenji Bhowji or some such. But a Madrasi name was no easy thing to get. Fortunately, the papers were at that time echoing the name of Mr. Chidamvaram Pillay. That was enough for the Pandit who said, "There it is. If Chidamvaram does, Viswamvaram may stand as good a chance. As for the title, well, find out some blooming cognate of Pillay, say liver." (Pillay means "spleen" in Bengalee.)

CHAPTER VI

OUR DAYS were passing through a thousand trifles and inanities when suddenly we had a gay flash of luck. The jail authorities passed orders to the effect that we could be removed from 44 Degrees, and penned together in one fold. This sent us into a perfect frenzy of joy, and it took us one good hour to sober down to a sense of our real position. The new quarters consisted of three rooms, more or less opening into one another. The one in the middle was large enough, while the wings were made up of two small cabins. Devabrata and Arabinda were allowed the occupation of the two wings, as they were rather serious sort of people. But the central hall became the den of the entire lot of the frivolous youngsters, who began to raise the devil there of all nights. Srijut Hemchandra Das of Midnapore happened to be one of the last batches. I had had no opportunity of knowing him before. But once I got thick with him, I found him to be of that class of people in whom the child is never dead. Hemchandra had that delightful combination of gray hair, mature intelligence and eternal childhood, and so rose much higher than the average. In a short time, he became an object of general love and respect and came to be called "Hemda" or "Big Brother Hem".

The two wing rooms echoed all day with religious studies and academic talks, while the central room was vocal with all manner of jocund din. Ullaskar was with us, and he kept things going in a merry whirl that left us not a single moment to grow glum over the impending fate. But the cup was yet to be filled and it was filled when the Police dragged in a new lot to roost in the sanctum of the Alipur jail. It would have been a repetition of the Black Hole Tragedy to put so many of the 'anarchists' into three small rooms. So once again the kind authorities vacated a big ward and accommodated us all there.

To the joy of happy accommodation were added those of another kind. Repeated complaints about the famous Regulation diet induced the Doctor to allow foodstuffs to be brought from outside. Sushil Sen's father would often send us fruits and sweets. The boys of the "Anusilan Samitee" of Calcutta occasionally presented us meat and things necessary for cooking it. Big Brother Hem, who was a master of all arts, would go to the Hospital ward to cook the thing for us. So often we had right royal dishes. Fruits would often come in in such large supplies that we could not use them all up, and had to make playthings of them.

The evenings were the most enjoyable of all hours of the day. After nightfall we had a regular musical soirée. Hem, Ullas and Devabrata had good voices. But Devabrata was of a grave turn of mind, and would occasionally only be won over to sing. One of his songs I still remember. It was a thing he had himself composed to celebrate an All-India Revolution. His deep bewitching voice, and the winged sense of the song visualised a blood-red scene where Revolution was stalking in a just passion. The following lines have survived all the lapses of my memory :

"The mighty Mother stood up, and millions of Her children gave the battle-cry... Blood covered up the Sun, and the stars and the moon had a bath of blood. The offerings were of blood, and the libations they poured were blood. The whole of the Earth burst forth into an unspeakable purple glory."

The song conjured up before the mind's eye an awful picture of a new India. In the background of it, was planted the gold throne of the goddess of India's destiny with sky-kissing breakers of a bloody sea heaving, plunging against it, and in the foreground were millions of people who had come from all this land between the Himalayas and the seas, and who, roused up by a touch of the goddess, and maddened by some sublime emotion, broke out into a war-cry that sounded like the roar of a hundred thousand lions, while the Heavens and the Earth seemed to resound with the din of battle.

For a few seconds we were deluded into the belief that we were free and entirely above all mortal fears. The boys sang popular patriotic songs of the time. They were uncontrollable in their effusions and their energy knew no exhaustion. The most remarkable of the lot was Sachin Sen. He had been once a student of the National College against the better wishes of his parents. But he soon found the college curricula so boresome that he gave them up and joined us. Such spirits were not to be easily let down. His wild ebullitions, his songs and oratorical exercises soon made the jail intolerable to us and the authorities. The jailor, who was a good soul, was not a little embarrassed by his boisterous charge. He was uncomfortably placed between a long period of service well within sight of a pension and a sense of delicacy in his treatment of us. A fourth wife at an age which might be on the wrong side of fifty and the nightly roaring music of our tuneful boys made life a hell for him. So, one morning, he walked up to us and said, "My dear sirs, would you please keep the boys a bit in order? You see I have to sit up all night because of my precious wife, damned mosquitoes, and these musical boys. If this goes on, I clearly see there's no chance of my living a year or so to be pensioned off. Yes, I shall lose the pension." This was a mighty reason for the boys to cry halt. We accordingly rattled out to the boys some wise "saws and modern instances", and sought to rub into their careless brains the blessed-ness of charity in the style of Portia. But the young ones had no kidney for good and profitable things. If they had, would they fall into the wickedness of fighting for the freedom of India?

The merry party would occasionally absorb even Devabrata, Arabinda and Barin, who were rather in no vein for it. The last one seemed to have broken down under a rude shock after the arrest, for he would always lie between his blankets perfectly indifferent to what went on around him. Devabrata awoke in the morning to sit cross-legged in his corner till 10 o'clock. After the meal, he would either sit silently till four or five in the evening, or would read the *Gita* or the *Bhagavat*. Arabinda would also keep his corner and get lost in his spiritual meditations. Even the hell of the noise that the musical boys made did never disturb or affect him. In the afternoons he would pace up and down the room, and read the Upanishads or such holy things.

A few of us like Kanailal would have their share of sleep

just after it had been dark, and get up at about eleven o'clock in the night, when the others had fallen asleep. Then they would rummage the beddings of all for sweets or fruits or biscuits. If the search failed to bring forth anything, they would fall into a fit of disappointment and end their exploits in some practical jokes. Often the boys would awake to find the tail-end of one's piece of cloth tied round the hands of another, or to see the ear of one of bound to the leg of another with a piece of cord. One night I chanced to awake at about 1 A.M., and found Kanai dancing a waltz in an ecstasy of joy with a tin of biscuits he had managed to rifle out of the beddings of somebody. The joyful demonstrations roused Arabinda who was sleeping close by. But Kanai at once slipped some biscuits into his hands, and Arabinda at once buried his face in the blankets, and gave no hint of a disturbed sleep. The theft remained undetected.

Sundays were the visiting days, and brought us not only additional joy, but also the news of the great outer world, and presents from friends and relations. Occasionally, the joy was crossed by a deep tragic strain. One day, Sachin's father came to see his child, and asked about the kind of food we had. Sachin replied, "Lapsi"; but to save the feelings of his parent he defined it as a very sweet delicacy! I had no idea of how the poor father felt; but later on, I chanced to have a bit of experience. Once my relatives came on a visit and had with them my own son just a year and half old. I was possessed with a keen longing to take him in my arms once before I was lost to him forever. But these iron-bars ! They stood mocking in the way. I felt in my inmost heart the grim soul-crushing nature of the prisons.

But to return to the story. In the course of time our case came up for trial, at the magistrate's Court, Alipur. This was very agreeable relief to the jovial monotony of the jail life. When we were driven through the streets, we saw a mighty course of people and quite a bustling stream of life. The Court itself was teeming with the men of the bar, and a sense of curiosity seemed to have inspired all men and things. But we hardly took any notice of what hung round the case. The trial itself was a sort of huge farce. The varied evidence and depositions full of ugly half-truths sent us laughing home. Never did we have a thought of the mighty importance of the case on which our lives hang. When the day's trial was done, we were driven home to the jail like a boisterous pack of boys after the school hours. Then at candle-light, Ullas would entertain us with proper learned discourse on the Anglicised Bengalee used by Mr. Birly [District Magistrate of 24 Parganas] in cross-questioning or on the chances of a mouse or a cockroach biting off the ends of the Court Inspector's moustache.

I have mentioned Narendra Gossain of Sreeram-pore a few pages back. What we had suspected of him came to be stoutly supported by facts. Within a day or two of the opening of the trial, he stood on the dock as an approver. His deposition led to further arrests and searches, and the Police ran on the track of those fictitious revolutionaries whom Hrishikesh had created from his fertile brains. For fear of violence from us on his person, Naren was removed from our company and lodged in the Hospital ward under the supervision of European warders. The authorities were very well obsessed with the idea. One day, the jailor said to us, "Look here, my dear sirs, I am afraid I shall founder within sight of the coastland. It was a piece of bad luck that threw you in my way just when I am going to enjoy a lovely pension in a year or so. What a relief it would be to get you safely off my hands! God forbid that having skipped my ship pretty safe near the haven, I would be done by the few remaining miles of water." But the irony of Fate! His fears were the shadows that coming events cast before them.

The case was committed by the magistrate to the Sessions,—a thing which meant long holidays for us. We had no earthly thing to do, and so tried to be as much jolly as we could. We would often try to settle the issues of the cases between ourselves. Some were for whole-sale hanging or acquitting. Once Kanai Dutta broke out, "My lads, there's no such thing as acquittal for you. You can get twenty years of jolly good life in the Andamans if that pleases you." Sachin protested. He set himself to demonstrate that India was sure of being free by that time. Kanai sat gravely listening to it for a short while, and then remarked, "I can't stake anything on this prospective Freedom of India, boy. But I shall cut my own way to Liberty and I simply can't afford to do twenty years in the jail."

We didn't look behind this light assertion of a very deep-felt resolution. But two or three evenings after this, he gave out that he had a sharp pain in the pit of his stomach, and was ill. The doctor called on and ordered his removal to the Hospital, where Satyen of Midnapore had been living as a victim of phthisis.

Then one fine morning when we were busy with our morning washes, we heard the reports of two distinct shots from the direction of the Hospital. Instantly we saw prisoners and warders all racing that way from all sides. We couldn't know for a long time what the row was for. Some said it was the Sepoys at target practice, and others that it was a fight going on inside the jail. Then came a compounder from the Hospital reeling like a drunkard, and fell forward on his face by the door of the jail-office-room. The blood had left the face of the poor fellow, and no words of what he had meant to say came out through his parched lips. Some fifteen long minutes passed in a heavy suspense till an old jail bird strode up and said, "Naren Gossain is no more."

We demanded what he meant.

"Why, sirs, Kanai Babu has quieted Naren by punching him with a few shots! If you go up to the Factory House, you will find Mr. Gossain measuring his precious length on Mother Earth. The jailor had also a close shave. He just had wits enough to shimble under a bench of the Factory House to get beyond the shots."

Soon the Alarm Bell went furiously ringing. All the warders ran towards the Hospital, and in a few seconds we saw Kanai and Satyen being led under a strong guard to the Forty-four Degrees.

CHAPTER VII

SIFTING FACTS and fancies, the substance of a possible true story was as follows:

Satyen whom phthisis confined to the bed in the hospital was once fairly haunted by the gloomy idea that he was doomed, and came to decide that there was nothing left for him to do in this life but to blow off the treacherous brains of Naren. This honest resolution of his somehow or other came to the ears of Kanai who, at once pretended illness, and got himself removed to the hospital. Then Satyen sent words to Naren to the effect that jail-life was quite an unbearable hell for him, and he was prepared to be a Government approver like Naren, but that he wanted to be well-tutored in the affair by the latter. Naren took it in good faith, and accompanied by a European warder came to interview Satyen. When they two were discussing the various complex points, Satyen suddenly whipped out a revolver and fired at Naren. The latter, while hastening to make good his escape, got only a slight wound in the legs. But the report of the shot was like a call to Kanai who had been somewhere downstairs, and who rushed up instantly.

The European warder tried to pull him back, but one shot was good enough to prostrate him with a yell. By that time Naren had left the hospital building—at the doors of which stood a Convict warder. But Kanai placed the muzzle on the breast of the warder and demanded correct information of the way Narendra had fled. The poor warder at once threw the doors open and pointed out the way. Kanai ran after Naren till he got his range, and fired at him three or four times. The reports brought all the jail authorities bustling on the scene; but none dared step out, and the dreadful appearance of Kanai made them all wheel back and melt like snow under sunshine, the jailor thrusting his huge bulk under a bench of the factory to the infinite amusement of all. Naren had by this time pitched forward on his face on the ground, near the gates of the factory house. When Kanai had exhausted all his shots the brave people of the jail hailed from all quarters with all kinds of offensive and defensive arms and got hold of Kanai. The incident broached a very puzzling question.

Whence did Kanai get his revolvers? The wise denizens of the jail suggested that the jack fruits or the tins of clarified butter we were allowed to have from outside must have imported them. Kanai gave out that the ghost of Khudiram who had been hanged in connection with the Muzzafarpore Bomb Case had secretly presented the things to him for punishing the traitor. But these theories did not seem to stand to facts. Spiritualists of even the Conan Doyle type cannot lend a countenance to such a story of ghostly- bootlegging. Even Indian ghosts who are known to do a lot of other unclean things have never shown such wisdom a second time. So, this theory must go down. As regards the "Jack fruits" or "ghee-tins" theory, —the Doctor always inspected these before letting them in, so there was no possibility of the revolvers coming that way. I think that it is not much of an impossible thing to smuggle in revolvers when things like tobacco and opium safely found their way in behind the back of the authorities.

But to pass from this point which need not detain us long. With this dire tragedy the spell of our good luck was suddenly broken. Half an hour after the incident, the Superintendent called on us with a large following, searched our persons and turned us out of the ward to get it searched. His men pocketed a few dibs that lay concealed under the bedsheets. Nothing actionable was found. Then the jail overflowed with the rank and file of the Police. There was a talk of dragging the tank of the jail compound for a few more possible revolvers. But though it held out to us the cheerful prospect of a few fish-dishes after a long abstaining period, it was never carried out into work. Then the Inspector General ordered us each to a separate cell—and we got back to our old familiar Forty-Four Degrees.

At sunset the jailor came with a long face. The gloom of disappointment hung heavy on him. He said in the bitterness of his heart. "My dear Sirs, if you had anything like this on your minds, why the devil didn't you choose some nice spot outside the jail? You are plainly desperate; why did you get yourselves arrested instead of getting blown off in a fair action?" We did our best to convince him that we had absolutely no concern whatever with the fatal incident; but he only smiled tragically and added, "You are at least sure of getting something to console you for what you have done. But you have ruined me, yes, clean ruined me, sirs," Shortly, in the Forty Four Degrees our jail life began with a vengeance. The old staff of officers was changed. The old Superintendent made room for a new one; the Doctor and the jailor got transfers; the Hospital closed its doors on us, and when ill, we had to rot in the cells. All communications among ourselves were prohibited. Outsiders were forbidden off. So, we were left alone to live out a course of a life.

Then the Indian warders were all replaces by Europeans; and two strong military squad were stationed in the jail to prevent us from escaping.

The first two cells in the row were fixed allotted to Satyen and Kanai. The rest of us changed our respective cells every five or seven days. When chance brought us into the neighbourhood of Satyen's or Kanai's cell, we managed to steal some bits of a conversation in the night time. Broad daylight would not favour such conversation. In the evenings, we were allowed to promenade in the jail compound, but never to get close enough to one another. It was absolutely hopeless to exchange even a few words without the warders knowing it. So, day by day, the agony of the prisons bit into the heart. There was no companion, not a god's creature to talk to. Only thoughts and thoughts—whirling, heart-eating, and brain-sweeping. One day I ventured to beg a readable book of the Superintendent, but he politely refused. The Government had left him no powers to exercise; he had only to carry out orders.

The cells in which Kanai and Satyen had been shut up never opened their doors. But one evening we found Kanai's cell unlocked, and made for it. To our surprise, the warders did not come frowning on us. A little later, we were told that Kanai was going to be hanged the next morning, and so the ban on intruding visitors was withdrawn.

We saw him and it was a sight one would have given his eyes to see. It is yet alive in my memory, and would be so for the rest of this mortal life. My strange fortunes had brought me in contact with many real saints. But I do-not remember seeing a face looking so godly serene as Kanai's before Fate gathered him to the House of the Dead. Not a line of cares, not a single shadow of grief or regret, not a twitch of unquiet could be traced in that face. It was like God's lily on the fields. I recollected once having met a Sadhu at Chitrakut who had told me that the most unmistakable characteristic of a real saint was his absolute apathy to life and death. Kanai was a living instance of that wise remark. He must have realised in himself the source of all that is good, abiding, and permanent, while this world with its horrors of the jail, its warders and gallows had become the faintest shadow. I heard that he had put on some two stones [put on weight], and I thought, "There must be more ways of knowing the eternal truth than the controlling of the senses known to old Patanjali. God is infinite, and his methods of manifestation in man must be equally infinite.

Then one glorious morning, Kanai was hanged. This British-ruled India had no room for him. But that is nothing to wonder at. The officers must have been puzzled by the happy, peaceful, looks of his when he rose to the gallows. A European warder edged up to Barin and whispered to him, "How many of this sort have you got?" How many? Well, the mad excited crowd that ran to offer the best flowers at the pyre on which Kanai had been burnt did amply show that much of that hero was still alive in the hearts of Young Bengal.

A few weeks afterwards, our case came up for hearing at the Sessions. We had again a taste of a new free life in open air. We had none of us money enough to fight the case; and so, it was arranged that the pleaders and the barristers for the defence would be paid as much as the funds raised for Aurobinda allowed. Those who could not go on with a lean fee soon gave back their briefs. At last, Mr. C. R. Das agreed to fight for us at a sacrifice. But it was such an inconvenience for the High Court practitioners to come down all the way to Alipur Sessions Court. So, they thought of getting the case transferred to the files of the High Court. This, if done, would also have given us the additional advantage of being tried by a Jury. Barindra, as an England-born, might have easily claimed all the high privileges of a full-fledged European subject of the Crown. But when the Judge asked him if he wished to claim these privileges, he stolidly refused. So, the case was taken up by the Lower Court.

This trial, like its predecessor, hardly interested us. The only thing related to it that pleased us was the regularity of very hearty lunches. The Regulation food had already turned into Dead Sea apples on our palates. So we prayed this suit might go on eternally like; the Bleak House Chancery suit, if it would keep on an unfailing supply of those lunches. When we were brought to the Court they used to put us in handcuffs and chains. If we had any occasion to go outdoors, we were dragged through the streets straddling like the spoils of Roman victories. This did not wound our feelings much, for we were scarcely people of dignity enough to get offended. But it raised our biles to see Arabinda dragged about like an ordinary felon. He himself did not much care for it though.

This case was only a repetition of the preceding one. It was all a sort of the Punch and Judy show to us. Often the singular depositions would throw us into convulsive roars of laughter. The Judge frowned, and bit his lips while the barristers would hasten to Arabinda with a request to keep the boys steady. But the latter would sit unmoved like a statue, and say in reply that he had no voice with the boys.

I remember but faintly things associated with the trial. The only exceptions are Inspectors Samsul and Abdur Rahman. The former had been appointed to engineer evidence against us. The part suited him like his skin. He knew more than others how to use soft words as very effective baits. Our boys had a song on him:

"My King's men love our old Samsul, By dogs, devils, and fiends! Though he to us is poison full, Like dogs, devils and fiends! We wonder, ay, we all wonder—When he be on beam-ends;—And neck and crop, comes howling down,—With dogs, devils and fiends."

Samsul got a lift after our case had been finished. But the weird sisters that work at the loom of life cut him off from the enjoyment of the lift rather cruelly. But the Court Inspector Abdur was the only bit of refreshing oasis in the heart of the burning sands of the Executive. He it was who brought us the lunches. I yet remember how his looks spoke a heartfelt sympathy as he thought of our grim futures.

But these outward things did not engross us much. We were then in the midst of raging factions among ourselves, factions that taxed us a good deal more than the proceedings of the trial.

CHAPTER VIII

THERE ARE people who club together for a definite common purpose, which served or eliminated, they again disband and split off. We were exactly like them. So long as there was the Revolution to hatch, it had been a star to guide us all along a common way. But after the arrest the star sank below the horizon of our life, and a centrifugal force steadily acted on us. Though all of us wished to see the blessed dawn of the Indian Independence, yet every-body had a particular theory of what the free Constitution would be like. To this cause of dissolution was added the bitterness of the failure of the entire organisation. In the leisured life of the jail, these forces of discord broke loose.

One party stood up for purely religious principles and became a butt for the pure politicians to sharpen their wits on. It was about this time that big brother Hem invented the phrase "spiritual miasma" to describe that metaphysical idealism which makes one quite unfit for all earthly business. Devabrata who belonged to the "Religious" class, would read long lectures on the deep mysterious problems of Religions, and talk glibly on metaphysical points while the big brother would write fancy distiches on the so-called champions of Religion. The prisoners' dock was a platform whence the propaganda work of each party started and got on wings. Barindra would occasionally shake himself into some interest in some spiritual questions; but for the greater part of the day he lay stretched in his own blankets in a full spirit of indifference. I had shares in both the companies, and managed to enjoy all the fun.

There was but one man among us who remained supremely above all these petty party-squabbles. It was Arabinda. We heard many strange stories about him from the warders. He was supposed to take no food, and many thought he had gone off his head. He allowed ants and cockroaches to eat at his dishes, and did such strange things as would never strike a sane man. I did often seek to find out the truth, but had never courage enough to question him. One day, I found his hair shining with oil. This was extraordinary and confounding, as we were not allowed oil. So, I made bold to ask him, "Do you have oil for your hair?" He stunned me with the reply, "I don't bathe." "But your hair looks shiny." "It does. But you see I am passing through some physical changes as I develop spiritually. My hair draws fat from the body."

I had noticed similar cases before, but would never understand them. Later, I saw more of this sort of wonders in Arabinda. Once I was seeing in the prisoners' dock when I chanced to look at him. I saw his eyes set like glass-balls. I had heard that the total suspension of the diverse functions of the mind, and its concentration on a single thing might produce a physical result of that kind. I at once called the attention of some boys to it. None dared approach him; and at last Sachin slided up to him and asked, "What have you got by your spiritual practices?" Arabinda put his hands on Sachin's shoulders and answered, "Why, my boy, the thing I looked for."

Then we shook off our timidity and collected round him for an account of his strange experiences. I could not follow him into all the wonderful mysteries of the inner life he talked about; but I plainly saw that this extraordinary man had turned a new corner in his life. He told us how he had got through the Vedantic system of culture, and was on his way to mastering the Tantric system, and how the last is an extremely difficult process. When asked where he had learnt the latter from, he replied, "A great Yogi visited me in the mental plane and initiated me into it." Then we asked him if he could divine the issues of the case wherein, we were involved. He said, "I shall be acquitted." His prophecy came true. A year's trial came to a close, and we got our sentences. Ullas and Barin were to be hanged. Arabinda got acquitted. Ten of us were to be exiled to the Andamans for life; and the rest got transportations or rigorous imprisonment for five or ten years. Ullas was apparently delighted. He came back with a flicker of a clear smile on his face and said, "Thank God, this dammed show is ended after all." The remark made a European warder say to his fellow warder, "Look here, the man's going to be hanged, and he laughs." The companion who was an Irishman replied, "Yes, I know; they all laugh at death."

It was in May, 1909, that the sentences were passed. All but a poor batch of some fifteen bade us a smiling farewell. We, too, smiled,—but the smile was heavy with the imminence of tears. Life seemed to get unbalanced all of a sudden, and black shadow hung over the Earth. Pandit Hrishikesh observed with all the resignation of the Vedantas, "Well, after all, life is but a wicked nightmare." The Big Brother plucked courage and said, "Never mind it. We shall pull through this too." I, too, tried to cheer myself up like the rest; but I am not of the stuff that goes to create a hero—and I felt it. To think that the rest of the life was to be sweated away in the prisons! Why, the gallows were a more welcome thing. My God! what a long price it was that I had to pay—and that to the last farthing. My mind began to look helplessly back through *time*. I saw that for some years past I had never thought of God as a poor mortal should. When in my young days I had ventured out as a sadhu, I had got much of a true faith in God. But all that simply died after my initiation into Vedantic metaphysics by a Swami Sarupananda in the monastery of Mayavati. I yet vividly remember the fatal day when my God was clean shot to death by the barbed logic of the Swami. My blood had come down to the freezing point, when I thought that alone and helpless, I would have to swim my way across the icy cold waters of this Ocean of Maya in order to reach the unchangeable state of beatitude. The idea that self-realisation meant a sort of unalterable state of trance, of an unbreakable suspension of the senses that do not break out into earthly desires, did not stick to me long enough. I gradually came to doubt if man could ever stand by anything as the ultimate truth; and I said to myself, "This self-realising trance and the full-blooded sensuous life are possibly but two forms of an Eternal Life which is infinite in its expressions. So, there's no earthly or unearthly good in denouncing this worldly life, and running after the trance. The active life was at least as good as the inactive trance." So, I gave work the highest place in life when I joined the Nationalist movement. Later, when Mr. Lele arrived with his doctrines of love and meditation, we simply laughed at him like so many wise snobs. Yes, if all life was but the expression of the same Divinity, there could be no sense in silent meditation. Mr. Lele scarcely said anything after that. His only remark was, "If you have understood what you say, you can safely ignore what I tell you. But are you sure you have understood?"

And yet when in jail I was cut off from all works, my life lost its steerage. I looked out for a support, and my mind called out in dark despair, "Save me, my God, save me."

But my misfortunes now gave me more than one opportunity to know myself. The judgment passed, we were all locked up in separate cells—in the midst of the grinding pressure of absolute loneliness. The brains very often seemed to be ripped open by the brooding, multiplying thoughts for an outlet. It appeared at times that I stood not long off from stark madness. The effects of this self-immersed life can be judged from the following narration. One night as I was sitting in my cell, a boy in the adjacent cell burst out into the freedom of a song, which had no pretensions either to correct tune or timing. But it struck me at an angle that threw me into a violent spasm of unreasonable laughter, and I roll myself on the floor. This cured me of a splitting headache. The song in the meanwhile had brought the warders running on the scene and the next day the luckless singer got penal diet.

The boys indulged in many fanciful things to save themselves. A boy broke a piece of lime off the walls and wrote on the doors of cell, "Long live Kanailal!" He had four days of penal diet. To this torture was added the malice of the warders themselves, who with but a few honest exceptions, tried to make fun at our cost. The honest and the sincere souls pitied us and felt for us. One of them actually smuggled in plantains for a boy who was on penal diet and carried off the skins in pockets. But the rest were always on some pretext or other annoying us. A big, burly Highlander played his bullying role a bit too far. We nicknamed him, "The Ruffian Warder". The fellow would often read lectures on the nobility of the English mission of civilising India. But it was the Chief Warder who rose head and shoulders above the others. He would often give us right English sermons—genuine Sunday brand, and extended to us hopes of some room in the Paradise whereto the English had always a right of entrance, provided we kept to loyalty. The Paradise of the British People! Why it beat all things hollow. One can put up with all the heartless tortures and insults of the jail, but a sermon from a British warder is the last pull the string can endure.

Hemchandra was clever enough with the palette, too. He would manufacture paints with moss, lime, and powdered brick, and etch beautiful figures on the cell-walls. He had to bribe the warders with curious paper-figures, made with his finger nails.

The solitary life of the Jail afforded favourable conditions for the cultivation of fine arts. Those who had no genius for the canvas would divert their talents to poetry. One day I found on the walls of a cell a poem by some "mute" Gray:

"The picking of the jute tells on the health And the bloom—it is gone! The warders are all villains with no sense They curse us all day long!"

We had to pick jute at that time. Occasionally some really fine lines would meet eyes. Though I am a sort of Jacob Doodlecalf for poems, yet the following lines still linger! in my memory:

"The twin roses of Radha's feet Have got the Infinite in lovely meshes Ten Thousand worlds heave up and flash—All in a whirl of conscious gladness."

The pity of a man's life ! It rushes out of the jails to knock itself against the rosy feet of Radha.

Meanwhile our case had been up in the High Court on an appeal. The revised judgment was pronounced in November. There were few reversals or alterations. Only Barin and Ullas got "transportation for life" instead of having to be directly led to the gallows. There was also reduction of terms in some cases too. The authorities stopped us from twisting coir-ropes lest we would use them to bilk the law by hanging ourselves. And in a few days, all but those booked for the Andamans, were sent off to do their sentences in different jails. We in our turn, sat in expectation of the transport ship.

CHAPTER IX

ON THE eve of our transportation, the C.I.D. people once more put in their official noses. This time the bait was the promise of a reduction of the penal terms served on us. This was temptation enough to make one shell out a secret or two. But they had already known so much of us that nothing remained beyond them. Yet they tried to feel if anything still eluded their omniscience; and for that purpose, they sought to exploit our painful prostrated state of the mind. They knew well that a solitary prisoner would die to have somebody to talk to; and they wanted to make capital out of this piece of knowledge. Yes, a month or two of solitary prisons makes one mad enough to speak to rats and cockroaches, not to speak of the C.I.D. people who are after all human beings. Then there is the possibility of leaking out one or two really important words in the heap of idle talk; and a systematic conversation carried on with some thirty of this sort of prisoners may be well expected to throw out a considerable number of workable hints. That was what those sagacious people counted on. Our organisation had a very dangerous loophole.

It was the lack of proper method. This might have been due to inexperience and insufficiency of funds. In European secret societies the different branches are captained by different men, and the members of one branch are never allowed to know those of others unless there is some special call for it. The Chiefs always sought to separate one branch from the others more or less completely, and thus save the whole thing going down in a crash if a particular branch fakes. But circumstances prevented us from doing this methodically. To make it worse, we had never checked our gossiping habits. All these combined to make the different secret societies yield one or two informers for the Government. Party jealousies and petty individual grudges did also a lot harm. It is no wonder that a race unused wield real authority for centuries would have leaders greedy enough for arrogating all powers to themselves, and thus giving birth to discontent and ill-feelings.

The C.I.D, people got nothing new, and they turned their back on us in despair. We had yet some time on our hands. But it was pleasure enough that other races have as good jaws as ourselves. The European warders had to keep their stations within the jail all the day long, and were not without their factions. One party would seek our alliance to get better of the other, and their gab would often let out a good deal of very startling jail secret.

Then one day came the notice that the Civil Surgeon would soon drop in for the medical examination of the prisoners. This meant that the berths were ready for us on board the transport ship. The Surgeon came on all right and found all fit except Sudhir and myself. We had dysentery and so we got to wait for some time more. According to the Prison Regulations we were to stay over three months longer. But for us the Regulations had no blessed value. We were started in six weeks; and I took what seemed to be a last glance at the dear native land from the jail.

One daybreak they put the handcuffs on, and got us two to enter the Black Maria. A couple of sergeants sat on either side of each, and the Black Maria drove straight to the Kidderpore docks. On board the Steamer one of the sergeants said, in jest, "Now say, 'My Native Land, farewell'." We laughed into his impudent face and said, "Au revoir." But in our heart of hearts we had not the slightest spark of a hope that we would ever come back. We were the only two political convicts on the ship, Sudhir and myself, and were put in a corner of the hold, which had been filled with other classes of convicts. An officer of the ship who used to send photos to some English journal came down, and wanted us to sit for him. It was something to be photoed for little more than a bare song. We "brushed up our turbans and put on our best looks. But we soon found that the maintenance of the best face did not give us anything better than three handfuls of fried rice (*chira*) for food. Sudhir, who was quite a big fellow, rebelled at the thing. A Mussalman of the Punjab who belonged to the Police said, "If you have no objection, you may share our dishes, sirs." This generous offer covered also a sinister motive of making converts of us. We replied, "Thank you. We are fully sure of our Hinduism, and so accept your offer." There were some Sikh Havildars who apparently thought that we were about to sell ourselves for a mess of pottage. So, in an exuberance of charity they came forward to offer us food. We obliged both parties, though the Sikhs thought that we Bengalees were not faithful and strict

Hindus. We do not presume to know if these were right, but we were saved from starvation that time. A number of Bengalee Mussalmans of Noakhali were on board, who offered us boiled rice, and a gourd dish. These tasted agreeably.

It was on the fourth day that we sighted Port Blair. The place looked lovely from a distance. Long rows of cocoanuts with straggling bungalows of the Europeans peering through them here and there appeared like a picture in frames. As yet the soul of the station was unknown to us. A sepoy pointed his fingers to the piles of a three-storied house and said, "There's the jail building. You shall go to that destination." Soon the boat slung into the port. A Doctor came up and examined us all. Then we were landed with our kits on the shoulders, and marched to the clang of the fetters.

A little dapper white man looked us up and down as we entered the jail, and said, "So, you are here at last! Well, you see that block yonder. It is there that we tame lions. You will meet your friends there, but mind you, don't talk."

We in our turn measured him with our eyes. Height 5 ft., breadth 3 ft., or thereabout. The man looked like a Homeric frog in modern European gentleman's habits. It was yet too early for us to know that he was the redoubtable Mr. Barry, the only authoritative hinge on which the jail life of the Andamans turned. He had the face of a live Bull dog, and he looked every inch one of those special creatures born to ride convicts. God must have certainly taken particular care to make this man everyway fit for his post at the Andamans. He invariably reminded one of Legree of Uncle Tom's Cabin. Time allowed us many opportunities to read this great man better, for we lived under his blessed government for eleven long years.

A Roman Catholic, and an Irishman, his religion concerned him only one day of the year. He sinned recklessly all the year round by thrashing convicts. But on the holy day of Christ's birth, he went to the Church to lay down his burden of sins at the sacred feet of his Confessor, put on peaceful looks, and would never kick a single convict. But for the rest of the year, he was always closely running down the convicts like Death.

But the convicts gave him an unfeigning testimony of virtue. I have always marked a peculiar trait in all convicts that they are fascinated by the iron man. Many a convict would remark after a good thrashing from Mr. Barry, "The villain is a piece of a man, after all." Milksops the convicts detest with all their vehemence of feeling. Under Mr. Barry's regime, if a convict stood supplicating his pity in the name of God, and asking his pardon for a piece of blackguardism, Mr. Barry would say, "This jail is my Province. There is no God to interfere with my absolute rights. I have been here for thirty years, but have never seen God encroaching on my territory."

These words were perfectly true, even though it was Mr. Barry who spoke them.

The first thing that arrested our notice was the promiscuous assemblage of races. Port Blair seemed to be the common meeting ground of people hailing from all the Provinces of India and Burma. The Mussalmans were equal in number with the Hindus, and the Burmese too had collected intolerably large figures. In India, the ratio of the Mussalmans to the Hindus is 1: 5; a fact which compared with their numerical equality in the Andamans must be explained by some racial characteristic. In Burma the population is only a quarter of what Bengal contains; but in the jail, there were more Burmese than Bengalees. The former having lost their independence only a few years ago have not yet been as meek as the Indians, and so are always up to some sort of riot and murder. There were mostly low class people of the Hindu sect. Madrasi Brahmins were very rare, a fact which might be due to either diffusion of education or milkiness of nature. When we reached the spot, we found the Pathans had already got the whipping hand, and were playing the bully.

All over the place there was a singular travesty of justice. Convicts of all classes had the same kind of treatment meted out to them. The nature of a man's crime had very little to do with the character of the work on which he was put. When the cocoanut coir was the article in demand, all hands were set to it; and if there was a demand for oil, cocoanut or mustard, every convict was engaged in the oil-pressing machine. The lord who ruled the whole show was Mammon. The convict was the cheapest labour the Government could have to the advantage of its coffers. There is always an article in the Government Jail Regulations that speaks of the differential treatment of prisoners, yet that scarcely weighs with the jail officials, whose only look-out seems to be to increase the income from the Jail Department. So out on the islands there, they did not care a hang for the health of the convicts. There was always a prospect of fresh batches of slaves to be sent over at a call, so long as there would be even a handful of European magistrates dominating the sources of supply in India.

Once I came across a man there. Poor soul, he had been from the district of Burdwan, and was a sweeper in the jail. The man had not a blessed idea of whence he had come, or why? I asked him, "How many brothers are you, my man?" He replied "Seven". "Do you remember their names?" He counted them by the joints of his fingers and gave five names, and then stopped short. I again said, "The rest, man?" He looked helpless like a child, and said, "I don't remember, sir." The man had never regular meals. Often he would sit speechless for hours or would be sweeping the place all the livelong day. One did not have to do much thinking to see that he would be more suitably confined in an asylum. But a wise judge it was who had thought him fit for the Andamans!

Occasionally though, one would chance on a clever fellow who shammed madness. I saw a Bengalee convict playing the role of a mad man to his advantage. One day the fellow smelled bad luck, and broke out into a wild song. He made a turban of his clothes, made his eyes look bloodshot by putting a bit of lime into them, and talked at random. At meals, he kept his face off the dish. The warders led him to the jailor who tested him with two plantains. The man ate up these without taking care to throw off the skins. So, the jailor concluded that the fellow had really gone off his head, or why the deuce did he swallow the skins which everybody cast away? When the man returned to the cell, I asked him, "Why did you swallow the skins?" He promptly replied, "I couldn't help it, sir. That d—d jailor had to be fooled. One can't be mad unless he takes some pains for it."

CHAPTER X

THERE IS an adage in Bengalee which defines hard lot as "kicks when you are on your legs, and blows of the broomstick when you are sitting". The full sense of this adage came home to us in the jail life in the Andamans. On our arrival, those of us who had been Brahmins had to give up their sacred threads. Such was the peculiar rule of the jail, though, clearly it was an interference with our religion. Curiously enough nobody cared to meddle with the symbolic beard of the Mussalmans, or with the long hair of the Sikhs. It was the Brahmin who was the victim of this liberal spirit. The reason was mighty simple. The Mussalmans or the Sikhs were dangerous people to play with, while the Brahmin was more or less inoffensive. The world never pardons the weak, and rejoices at the cost of those who do not grumble to pay. Be that as it may, we quietly yielded the innocent symbol of our powerless caste, got into the regular flock, and settled down to live on the Regulation food. This required no small amount of grit, for the food was more hopeless than what we got at Alipur. One can somehow or other manage with coarse Rangoon rice and equally coarse home baked bread; but the most famished Bengalee youth would pause before a dish of arum, green and unpeeled plantains, and Indian spinach all boiled into a horrid mess along with gravel and rat's muck. But we had been used to all sorts of things before, and so we lived on the dish without much discomfort.

All conversation between ourselves was tabooed under penalty, and we were allotted to a block where the Madrasi and the Burmese elements predominated.

The works we had to do were no easy things. They got plenty of cocoanuts in the place—all government property. The local industry was one of cocoanuts. The convicts were generally put on coir-pounding, rope-making and oil-pressing. There was a cane-factory where young boys worked. The worst jobs were the hammering of the coir and the crushing of oil. Barindra and Abinash were the weakest of us, and they were engaged in making ropes, while all the others were put on coir-pounding. This work began soon after a scanty breakfast of "kanji". Each got the dry husk of 20 cocoanuts, which were to be placed on a bit of wood and thrashed with a wooden club till they were flexible enough. Then the hard outer skin was pulled off and the coir softened with water for further thrashing. The last process separated the dust from the simple fibres which were then dried in the sun. Every one of us had to get two pounds of these fibres per day.

It took us a large part of the first day to see into the job, and when after that we took up the club, it gave us painful blisters in the palm of the hand. A full day's close-tipped labour yielded only half a pound of fibre. At 3 o'clock I went to report the outturn, and was quite confounded by the amount of savage grimace they made at me, and the blooming language they used on me. And the tongue they had! It would be more to the point to call it a blessed razor. I have read in a Bengalee novel by Mr. Sarat Chandra Chatterji that the upcountrymen of India have the sharpest and longest tongues, but I would humbly request the great author to try the language of Port Blair. It fascinates all those who have the luck of its acquaintance for it is an ever-refreshing spring of joy rising out of the curious blend of Hindusthani, Pathani, and Beluchi. The cadgers of our country who are quite authorities enough in the use of garbage cannot hold a candle to the masters of the Andamans Babel. I never knew that there were so many forms of abomination, and was never used to accept insult or such a language without paying back something harder. But now there was no remedy. One evening as I sat gloomily in my cell after a long day of rather tiring work punched with insulting remarks from the petty officer, a Pathan warder asked, "What's the matter with you, sir?" I related to him all that had happened. He listened quietly and then said, "Sir, this is my fifth year here. I have seen people who sulk and brood over this sort of things. They either go mad or get hanged for some row. So you had better shake it off. God may mend this, sir, in time." The name of God struck me agreeably. It is when men get hopelessly adrift that they think of God. This may account for the rather longish rosaries the convicts used in taking God's name. We first laughed at this showy piety of theirs, but were soon convinced that it was no laughable thing. A man calling on God even in his distressful moments may be pious.

With passage of time, however, things grew worse. It is so much easier to go straight to the gibbet than to die by inches. None was known to have returned alive to his home after having had to serve a life sentence out in Port Blair under section 121 of the Indian Penal Code. According to the Andaman and Nicobar Manual a life sentence meant solid twenty-five-years with a future at the mercy of the Government. Surely it was easier to hang ourselves with a piece of a rope than to pass our whole life in the Andamans. But perhaps I had not yet reached that desperate condition of mind in which death looks so welcome.

We shuffled through our days somehow or other. But the little lords of the jail made our life almost unbearable. The whole host of petty officers, Tindals, and Jamadars had many privileges and small powers. They were all of them convicts whose service in the jail had raised them to the posts of warders and petty officers. A humorist and orator once said to us in our young days that a "teacher" is one who uses the "terrorising birch". We thought of it in the jail there, and saw that a "warder" is one who can work the rod on all luckless fellows. Anyway, the rod and the warder were inseparably associated. The method of discipline was charming: "That fellow Ramalal there has moved out of the file; just knock him back into his place"; "there Mustapha did not stand up immediately he was told; pull him up by the moustache". "Bakhaulla there has been an age to the lavatory, let him have three blows on the back so that he may look sharp in future";— so ran the contrivances whereby these limbs of authority would keep jail-life in motion and order.

Some convicts often concealed money in a pouch they made in their throat; but the warders always tried to find them out and claim a share. We had no money to bless us with; so, we could only with great difficulty appease them. Barin had a poor allowance of 12 oz. of milk from the Hospital because he had a very feeble health. But he had to purchase his safety by offering his share to the Petty Officer, Khoadad Miah, who was a fiercely orthodox Mollah, and an absolute God's man. He drank up the milk in an appreciative style, and said, "My God! what a thing He has made there!"

All this was more intolerable because there could be no appeal to higher authorities for redress. The weak, therefore, had no chance in the jail as outside it for justice. Convicts generally had no heart to complain against these petty tyrannies, and nobody would run useless risks for others. If anybody would be rash enough to lodge a protest, he had to back it up with sufficient evidence or he was sure to get a worse licking for false imputations. Honesty was the last thing that could be regarded as paying. Only those men who could fawn with a tongue in their cheek and tell unmixed lies were sure of winning a good name and creeping up into official good books. But those who had the hardihood of standing up for a just cause would be fast driven to the walls.

This precious process ended in hardening all hearts against so called systems of justice. The jails of the British Government do not reform character, and in ninety-nine cases out of a hundred they drive a man furiously to lowest depths of criminality. In our days at Port Blair the authorities had no ideas of reforming criminals. For them, the convicts were working machines and the competency of an officer was measured by the turn-out of these human machines under his particular supervision.

I well recollect an eventful day. From morn till nightfall I sweated but never succeeded in turning out the required quantity of oil which was thirty pounds. I felt dead tired and things just danced before my eyes. To this was added a mind already embittered by the insults of the supervising warder, who at the end of the day conducted me to the jailor. The latter treated me like a dog, and bestowed on me an intolerably flowery language, clinching his famous admonition with threats of flogging. I returned to my cell and to my meal. But there was such a big lump somewhere down the throat, and a heart-breaking sense of misery and rage had seized me. A Hindu warder noticed it and said, "Well, this gentleman here is troubled in the mind. Let him have a good dinner." The words almost induced me to break out into a shriek, and I checked myself only by squeezing my throat with the hands. One could bear with kicks and blows; but pity!— it would break the heart.

Then the Pathan warders were arrayed against us under the impression that their only way to the official preference lay through whipping us to the heel. Accordingly, they made it their business to get us into odd scrapes. Innumerable trifles often were magnified into serious charges against us through their cunning engineering. One Sunday, while doing our allotted work of washing the building, I found Ullas a few yards off, and edged up to him for a bit of talk. But as soon as I called him by the name, a blow was at once landed on my back. I turned round, and took one more in the face. There stood before me the grim figure of Mohammad Shah, the Pathan Petty officer, who was thus doing the orders of the Government and maintaining the Jail discipline. On another occasion, this sort of zealous obedience was carried further. The oil-crushing business to which we had been appointed for a time came to an end with every blighting prospect of a revival. But the next time I openly revolted against it and said in unmistakable words that it would not be my job at all events. The authorities flew into a stormy rage and ordered me to a solitary cell and penal diet. This lasted till my health broke down, and I was again ordered to the coir-hammering. It was once during this work that I fell foul of a warder. The day was hot, and the work had taken away all my strength. Sweat was running down the body in streams, and the club wherewith I hammered the coirs bumped every now and then against my head. The thing was getting too taxing when I chanced to look out of the bars and saw a Punjabi Mussalman warder. I requested him to give me some water to moisten the hard fibres with; but he grimaced and said, "Damn it! I won't. Do the thing without water." My temper had been on its edge all that day, and so I replied, "What makes you grin like that? Say straight what you have to." The fellow took offence, and growled, "What! you ease your tongue against me?" It was too late to get back with credit, and so I rasped out, "Yes, I do. You are not above it like a blooming prince? Are you?"

He took me by the neck ring and gave such a rude jerk that I knocked my head against the iron bars, and was filled with such a blind rage that I could have hammered his noodle into a thousand pieces if he were within my reach. But as it was, the thing was out of question. Yet there was no ease for me unless I could give him something back. So, I seized his hand and bit it till it ran blood. The man went off to report to the jailor; but fortunately for me, he met a Hindu Petty Officer on the way who persuaded him with soft words and threats to keep silent.

Events like this occurred twice more; and I was at last forced to conclude that these warders were attracted to those who could give them a licking. The weak are always trodden roughshod, and the Pathans never let slip a single opportunity of persecuting the weak. But they have one remarkable excellence that outshines all other darker traits. When they accept one as a friend, they stick to him through rough and smooth. These people are more ferocious, but more courageous and steadfast than we are. During the strikes the jailor put these Pathans on us, but they often turned out to be our best friends; and in the endless splits of the jail people, we always tried to have the strongest allies.

The racial feelings were now and then very bitter among the Hindus and Mussalmans, the latter having always some preference for their co-religionists. That was the reason why these Mussalmans were always seeking to be in all posts conferring some privileges and powers on them, and to proselytise the poor Hindu convicts. Almost all Mollahs are actuated by an idea that God would grant them no end of bliss in Paradise if they could convert a Hindu. Accordingly, in the jail they never tired of coercing a poor Hindu into obeying the three cardinal rules of proselytisation, namely, accepting food out of the dishes of a Mussalman, pruning the moustaches, and repeating the sacred Formulas of the Koran. The Hindu convict would find many of the powerful Mussalmans plotting against him, and throwing temptations in his way. He would be told that he could be happy as a Mussalman and free from all tortures, if he gave in. Like these Islamic missionaries, the Arya Samajists would carry on a brisk propaganda work, inducing Mussalman converts to recant. The ordinary Hindu did not bother about it all. He knows only to eliminate, and never to assimilate. However, the feud of the zealous had a very remarkable result.

It brought into the limelight the Hindu symbol of the small tail of hair on the crown of the head and the Mahomedan symbol, the beard. Those low-class people of Bengal who are never in the habit of maintaining the abbreviated pigtail did get it there in the Andamans; while the followers of the Prophet qualified themselves for their Paradise by reading curious things like "Hanuman's fight with Ali", "Mahoment vs. Siva","Rimes on Sonavan Bibi", etc. As we took food equally with both the Hindus and the Mussalmans the rival parties were puzzled, and were forced to conclude that we Bengalees had no strict codes of a faith. At last, they called all political prisoners Bengalees.

The political convicts too had their schisms. As they increased in number, the splits were more and more sharp. Readers of Tolstoy's Resurrection know how the famous writer has analysed the revolutionary psychology; and I found all his observations to be scientifically correct by the light of our factions there. Common Revolutionaries never fail to over-estimate their individual capacities. They have always a larger dose of vanity and self-assertion than average people. That may be the reason why they go the unbeaten ways, ways fully dangerous. But I have always suspected that they do not have as much depth as surface, and are generally fanciful, short-sighted and neurotic. Whenever I chanced to come across a new political offender there, I always tried to discover if any of his relatives on the father's or the mother's side had been a victim of neurosis. Ten to one, my suspicions proved correct. My old friends may get offended by this remark of mine; but it is no use; for I am one of their old party, and my grand-mother was a bundle of nerves.

But the peculiar characteristics of a Revolutionary do not

have free play under pressure of work; but when the jail puts an end to all forms of activities, those characteristics break out in the shape of factions. In the Andamans jail, there was no end of petty squabbles about the comparative achievements of different political groups or of different leaders. Everybody stood up for his own particular party and abused the others, and all this narrowness of mind was always mixed up with gross provincial jealousy. "National India" and "Integral India" were used as mere veneer for any sort of stupid trash. The Maharashtra leaders conclusively proved that the Bengalee idea of Nationalism was exclusive and straight-laced by arguing that Bankim Chandra, the Bengalee novelist, had mentioned only "seven millions" instead of three hundred millions of Indians in his song "Bande Mataram", and that Dwijendralal, the Bengalee poet, had never looked beyond Bengal in his song "Bengal, my mother etc.". One Punjabi Arya Samajist did not scruple to denounce Raja Rammohun Roy as a traitor, simply because that Great Reformer had approved of English education in India. Such logic smacked of Bedlam, but it was used by very sane persons through blind jealousy. The Maharasthra leaders had this provincial antipathy more than others. They liked to see India governed by their people. The Hindusthanis and the Punjabis were so rash! the Bengalees had so much jaw, the Madrasis were timid and cowardly, so the only live people of India were the descendants of the Great Peshwas. This was the burden of all their talk.

CHAPTER XI

OTHER TROUBLES were in store for us. Pandit Ramaraksha of Punjab protested against the forced process of "fraternising", and refused to give over his sacred thread, symbolic of Brahminism. He told the jailor that his religion did not allow him to take food without the thread on and he would obey the tenet at all costs. This was no narrow orthodoxism, for the Pandit was a man of learning and experience. He had travelled far and wide, in Japan, China, Siam and other places. His protest was simply inspired by his sense of duty. But the weak have no voice. His thread was taken off and he went on hunger-strike. After four days of complete starvation, he had milk pumped into him through the stomach pipe. This continued for a month or so till he got phthisis, and was removed to the Hospital where he got the better of all jail and earthly governors by his death. The man had already suffered long in the Burma jails before his coming to the Andamans, and his health had since been failing. But his mettle was all right up to the last moment. Before his death, he fought a hard fight for a strike then going on in the jail.

In six months after our arrival, some twelve more political convicts came over from Nasik, Khulna and Allahabad, and made with us a party of twenty-two. But along with this first addition, came also a superintendent like a malignant comet in our sky. He soon employed some of us to press oil. The machine at which Ullaskar worked is something like what we get in the indigenous oil-trader's house, while those at which we worked were hand-machines. Every man had to turn out ten pounds of mustard or thirty pounds of cocoanut oil per diem. Even Jack Dempsey would find his wind go off like embers to work at this machine for some time; so our condition is easy to imagine. This department was also in charge of a Pathan petty officer, who on the first day of our admission there, explained to us, as he held his swarthy fist over our very noses, that he would smash our noses if we would not do our full bits. The prospect did not cheer us much; but it was no time to speculate. So off we went up to the second story, each with a 50 lb. sack of cocoanut on the shoulders and a big bucket in the hand. Then the work commenced. It was something like a heavy-weight championship fight. It knocked the wind out of us in some ten minutes and the tongue glued to the roof of the mouth. But there was no rest. One hour of the toil, and the limbs began to hang senseless about me. In a futile rage I showered curses on the superintendent, and thought of crying aloud for a relief. But it was so humiliating! When the bell for ten o'clock summoned us to our meals, I found the palm of my hands all blisters while stars broke out before the very eyes, and the ears were filled with indistinct drumbeats. Our old Hemchandra was sitting gravely in a corner. I asked him, "Well, my boy, how do you like this job?" He showed me his hands and replied, "Look here, my hands have become all wood." But the Big brother was a wonderfully strong man. He never gave in, even if his hands were wood, and was unequalled in his patience. He was not moved by any amount of hardship and torture, and was always determined to do the right thing in the teeth of intense sufferings. Whenever any of us was up to anything desperate, Hemchandra's unruffled optimism came to his rescue. Only two of us, Indu and Bibhuti, could do the required quantity of oil; and the rest had to beg help for it. A month passed by, as we went on slaving at the crushing machine by day time, and lying half-dead by night. Then there was a relieving change of hands. This succeeding batch of workers included Abinas who had been exempted from this business by the former superintendent on account of his weak health and a chance of tuberculosis. The new superintendent, Major Barker, sent him down to it without worrying about a medical examination. Sreeman Nanda Gopal, ex-editor of the "Swaraj" of Allahabad, was also one of the batch.

Nanda Gopal was a Punjabi Kshatriya. All tall, handsome man, convicted under section 124A of the I.P.C. He did a blooming startling thing as he went to press oil. He said at once that he was quite unwilling to work at a savage speed. So, he was allowed to work as slow as he could, and as a result he did less than a third part of the required quantity before he came down for his meal. According to rules the convicts got all the time from ten to twelve for the meals but they snatched hasty mouthfuls and in five or six minutes were back at their work. For the poor souls couldn't think of enjoying a rest before the allotted work was done. Nanda Gopal seemed to be bothered by no fears. The Petty Officer came on to bid him hasten up, but was told in reply that hasty meals tell on the digestive organs, and that he was not going to blackmail the government by hurrying into illness in the ten years that he was to live there. The Petty Officer was rather taken aback; and in a puzzled mood reported the case to the jailor who at once came thundering down. But Nanda Gopal was enjoying what he ate to the chagrin of the jailor, and the latter threatened to lick him if the required amount of work was not done. Nanda Gopal again gave the jailor all his hygienic reasons for a slow course and said all blandly that he was determined not to go against the Government rules that limited the meal time to two hours from ten to twelve, and that he would take care that the jailor himself did not violate the said rules. This left the jailor nothing but to retreat honourably under a cloud of strong words and threats. The meal finished, Nanda Gopal got back to his post, thus deluding the Petty Officer into a false hope of seeing some more work. But the Editor of the "Swaraj" peacefully spread on the floor a piece of blanket, and went to sleep. Not all the sharp shower of vituperations of the Petty Officer could disturb his sleep. The man was more than a master of Mahatma Gandhi in matters of Passive Resistance. At noon he got up, and worked at the machine till he pressed some fifteen pounds of oil. Then he put back the remainder of his share of Kopra into the sack and sat down to rest. But the work was only half-done, and who the deuce was going to do the remaining half? Nanda Gopal said, "I don't know. Anybody that likes is welcome. Only I am not going to press oil all day long like a bull. I don't get six pice worth of food daily; how the devil do they expect me to turn out thirty pounds of oil per day?"

This set the Governors by the ears. There was a tremendous

lot of roaring and bullying but all that did not affect Nanda Gopal more than a pin-prick. He kept on his cheer and spirits as much as before. At last, the Governors got hopeless of him and ordered him to be locked up till further orders and put him in irons. Meanwhile Abinas had broken down. He had scarcely fire in him after ten; and Indu, being the strongest of our lot, consulted other prisoners, and managed by joint labour to do the work for Abinas. A month was nearly out when the jailor made terms with Nanda Gopal. He was to do only four days of regular work, and would then be immune from labouring at the oil machine. Nanda Gopal agreed, and saved himself by doing the work with the help of others.

Yet he did not long enjoy his immunity. In a few days, he was again ordered to press oil. But he flatly refused and preferred irons and cell. We of the first batch had to go in again. This made us halt and pause. We had an unrelieved prospect of a life-long jail-life; and it was clear that the torment of oil-pressing would certainly be too much for us. We must see our way to some fixed terms with the Authorities respecting our works. All possible forms of punishment hang over us like the sword of Damocles; why should we then be the instruments of our own torture? We followed the example of Nanda Gopal and struck work.

The Authorities frowned, and plunged into a career of persecution. It was a grim festival that set in. One form of punishment succeeded another. The first came in the shape of 4 days of penal diet with seven days of standing hand-cuffs. The penal diet meant a pound of powdered rice thrown into some boiling water. A strict guard was put on us to prevent us from smuggling in any kind of food. The jail regulations did not allow the Authorities to force the penal diet on any convict for more than four succeeding days. But the Regulations were mere letters for us. Ullas, Nanda Gopal and Hotilal had to live fourteen days on this diet. In 1913, when Sir Reginald Craddock came to the place on an inspection, Nanda Gopal complained to him of this treatment. But the Authorities had taken good care not to enter all this in the Convict's ticket, and the jailor, too, unblushingly said that the allegation was false. A convict cannot prove, his statement against the jailor. However, along with all the possible forms of torture that can be made out of irons, came those of separate confinement. In this matter, too, we were treated with some distinction from the ordinary usage. The average prisoners were allowed to come down to their meals, and could even speak to their comrades. But we had no such liberties. So, we had solitary confinement, though the Authorities were pleased to call it separate confinement. So passed some three months or more.

All this resulted in making us break down, so far as physical health was concerned. Port Blair was a notoriously malarial place. One had the fever on almost every day of the year. This was soon aggravated by a new epidemic of dysentery. The Authorities, too, got tired of all the old forms of penalisation and thought that some change was necessary. So, we were sent to work on the settlement outside the jail. Barindra was posted in the Engineering Department; that is, he got to do a journey-man's work to any lucky mason; Ullas was put on brick-making; some were sent to the Forest Department, others to the drawing of rickshaws, and the rest to build up an embankment or some such thing.

But things had always a trick of turning out badly through

the perversity of our luck. Inside the jail the work was enough to knock us out; but we had a sufficient quantity of food, and protection from the rains or the blinding sun. Outside the jail, we lost all this comfort. From six to half past ten in the morning, and from one to half-past four in the afternoon, we had to work hard and were always exposed to a scorching sun or drenching rains; and Port Blair had the rains for seven months out of twelve in the year. To add to our misery, the Forests were full of leeches, which had driven numbers of men into desperate flights. Then a regular meal was a rare thing to get. A part of the allotted food was always sure to be stolen and sold in the villages. Everybody knew it, even the overseer and the ordinary convict. But seldom was the misappropriation brought to light or punished. The only reason was that all the Officers were more or less "facile" and sailed in the same boat. And the poor convicts dreaded the consequences of a protest too much to raise one.

There were other difficulties the Authorities were pleased to throw in our way of life. Of the four Hospitals, managed by Bengalee Assistant Surgeons, none would open its doors to us. This was by the order of the Chief Commissioner. So, when sick, we had to travel back some ten miles to the jail with our movables, —a thing which was no joke. The jail, too, offered no fair medical help. There were some small cells adjoining to the Hospital, and the back walls of these had a small window through which the rains could more easily splutter in than sun-rays or air. We had to live in these in our illness, and use the iron tubs they contained as lavatory. I am told that the Jail Commission that visited Port Blair in 1920 on an inspection rather strongly remarked against these cells. But that is beside my narrative.

After all this, our hopes of a free happy, outdoor life met their Waterloo in no time. It looked as if we had the prospect of Scylla and Charybdis. We had not even the luck of an ordinary convict and his promotions. So one after another all went back to the jail.

Then a tragic event took place. Indu Bhusan, who had been a strong man, and never smarted under the severest hardship hanged himself. Petty insults meted out to him had exhausted his patience. He would often say, "I don't think I would weather it out for these ten years of my life." One night he tore his shirt into shreds to make a rope which he fastened to a window high up in the back walls of his cell, and hanged himself. The superintendent was rung up in the same night, but he turned up only in the following morning. Those of the warders who entered his cell that night in the train of the jailor said that they had seen a piece of paper attached to his neck-ring. Only God can vouch for the truth of that, but no such thing was seen by us. We asked the jailor about it afterwards, but he denied its existence. An elder brother of Indu moved the Government for an enquiry into the affair, and the Deputy Commissioner of Port Blair was commissioned to it. But nothing came out. It was bungled up as usual.

This was followed by another mishap. Ullaskar was one of those who came back from outdoor work. He had been put in a brick-field. But the junior Medical Officer of the locality found him unfit to work in the sun. The white overseer did not care a hang for what a Bengali medical officer said, and sought to confine Ullas to the work. But the latter refused and returned to the jail with the remark, "I can't bring myself to work under threats of punishment, it kills my moral sense." He was punished with seven days of standing handcuff. But on the first day at 4-30 P.M. when the Petty Officer went to take off his hand-cuffs h1e5found Ullas drooping in a high fever. He was at once removed to the Hospital. The fever rose to 106° in the night; and when day broke on our dark convict world, Ullas was found to be completely changed, though the fever was off. The man who had kept an even temper through all the tempests of life, whose face had never darkened under the severest pain, was unhinged. Ullas had gone mad in a single night!

The jail looked on us in a terrible frown. So there was clearly not the ghost of a chance of our returning back to home alive! The grim gibbet or stark lunacy stood staring hard at us. Why should we then submit to all this torture? We took counsel, and decided to strike work till we had fair terms. But as soon as our ultimatum reached the Authorities, they began to think out a way of snubbing us.

The fight was a pretty bit of tenacious affair like those of the elephant and the crocodile in the folk- lore. Our party had a reinforcement by the arrival of Nanigopal of Chinsura, Pulin Babu of Dacca, and three or four others. Nanigopal was quite a lad; yet he was forced to join us by the despotism of the Authorities. We were separated from others and put in a separate block under the care of some select Pathan warders. Our rations were reduced and strong measures were adopted to prevent us from conversing with one another. We had not the free use of the lavatory even. But where the chains are stronger they snap the sooner; and people who have no love for the law can hardly be made to obey it under threats. When they put a ban on our communications by shutting us up in cells separated from one another by all the space of four or five cells, we fell shouting and hallooing to one another. Handcuffs cannot gag a man. By and by, the Authorities were in a fix. They had the incubus of a prestige which kept them from conceding our just demands while the strike persisted as long as they would not satisfy our demands. At this crisis, the old superintendent came back and displaced the new one. He consulted the Chief Commissioner a little, the latter caved in so far as to send us on easy jobs abroad on the settlement. We said we could agree to that if all of us were sent outdoors, otherwise we could very easily retrace our steps to the jail.

Some twelve of us were sent out to guard the cocoanut plantations, which were a valuable property of the Government. The job was not much trying; but we were disbanded and distributed over the wide area without any opportunity of seeing one another. But the Authorities played some tricks. They had not sent out all the political prisoners as stipulated. Nanigopal and Nanda Gopal had been only removed to the Viper Islands jail where the former again went on hunger-strike. This rekindled the strike inside the jail, and we, on the settlement, also stopped working. It took us a fairly long time to arrange the strike; for we lived far from one another, each ignorant of the whereabouts of the other. When we were sent back to the jail for three months the strike inside the jail had almost broken down. They brought back Nanigopal after four days of fast, and pumped in milk through the stomach-pipe so that he might live to the eternal glory of those who enforced discipline. The young fellow persisted in the hunger-strike even when all the others had stopped.

Day in day out, Nanigopal stuck to it and was emaciated

to the very skeleton. The officers did not scruple to keep him in handcuffs even when the boy had starved for a month and a half. The atrocity of this one thing led to a fresh general hunger-strike. At the same time the papers in India were ringing with the tragedies of Ullaskar and Indubhusan. The Government of India was at last forced to send Dr. Lukis to look into the affair; but the Doctor's report has not yet seen the light, though he got Ullaskar to be sent over to the Madras Lunatic Asylum and helped to bring some mitigation of our hard lot. The friends of Nanigopal too gained him over to take food. Those of us who had come to the jail for three months found their terms expired, and went outdoors.

CHAPTER XII

BUT WHOM the gods have abandoned, Death cannot relieve. We were passing our days through rough and smooth in the settlements when a report of some sort of agitation in the jail again upset us. It was to the effect that Nanigopal had again struck work under persecution. As a punishment they had tried to make him put on gunny cloth, which he refused. They, then, had forcibly divested him off his loin cloth, and ordered him to take the piece of gunny cloth; but he had stolidly thrown it away, and preferred nudity on the holy principle, "Naked we came out of our mother's womb, and naked shall we return." He broke his ticket into potsherds, did the Chief Commissioner no courtesy by standing up before His Honour, and refused to beg anything as a favour. We were at first afraid that he, too, had gone off his head. But on enquiries we found out that he was in full possession of his wits. What he troubled over was the propriety of obeying the laws and the courts of justice established by the British people without caring to consult the needs and grievances of the children of the soil. His own particular sense of justice did not approve of obedience to such laws and courts of justice, and he would not serve these only to keep his head on the trunk of a mortal body. One does not certainly find life worth much when it means a course of bitters only.

We could not find any solution to his doubts excepting the single one that when God stamps a soul with a longing for freedom, no earthly power, however armed and expert, can altogether crush it. Even the body that harbours such a soul cannot be shut up in any Bastille however strong and formidable.

Time brought about a vicissitude of fortune for us also. The Calcutta Press was rather strongly eloquent over the miserable lot of the Port Blair convicts. The Authorities took it into their heads that we were supplying the Press with the workable stuff. We had been for some time not overmuch lawfully engaged. Hunger would often drive us hither and thither in search of some eatables, and love of company would often lure us into clandestine meetings. But of the charge laid at our doors now we knew nothing. Yet the Authorities one day made a big fuss and surrounded our wretched barracks. This was such a farcical tag to the old Manicktala Tragedy! A very studious search resulted in nothing but the find of a few useless letters or poems. These, the Authorities thought, were enough. The Chief Commissioner packed us off to the jail where there was a very funny rumour afloat. Somebody had confidentially told the Chief Commissioner that we were all plotting to blow off the Island with bombs and to journey back to India in a Government steamer we had already nailed. His Honour, thus persuaded by Lalmohun Saha, his spy, got us safely in the jail and saved the Island. When he came to the jail, we humbly asked him, "Well, sir, what is all this fuss about? Why does your Honour deny us the sunshine of your favour?" His Honour replied like an honest soul, "Why, I don't know. I only act under the orders of the India Government."

The reply was above criticism. But shortly we heard that some outside people who had been familiar with us were being punished, and a witness had been actively engaged to substantiate the charge of conspiracy against us. We were further told that the jewel of a witness had unearthed some gramophone pins and iron splinters, things which, he said, would go to making bombs. We had learnt from the Naraingarh affair which has been the unhappy cause of many innocent people's undoing that the Police could do miracles. So we asked the Authorities, "If you suspect us or have anything against us, why don't you try us in open courts? What goose sense can there be in this sort of stealthiness?" But they gave a slight turn-up of their lips by way of a mysterious smile and stalked off leaving us perplexed.

A few months afterwards, Sir Reginald Craddock visited the jail. We thought of finding in him a blessed knight who is always sworn against injustice and tyranny, and resolved to bare our hearts to him. But as we got about it, the Chief Commissioner looked fire and growled, "You conspired against the Government there outside the jail." We said, "If so, why did you say that you knew nothing when we asked you about this? Why did you not let us have a fair, open, trial? Sure enough, you have evidence to go down in a court." Sir Reginald smiled a dignified king-like smile, and said, "Well—er,—you know this sort of thing can't be proved."

Nanigopal represented his case. The knight flared up with all the mediaeval indignation against disloyalty and said,

"You are an enemy of the Government; you should be shot." Nanigopal asked, "If so, why all this foolish show of law-courts and advertised justice? What's the good of wasting so much of good money. The thing could be done at less expense."

The inspection closed at this stage. There was no hope but God now; and he seemed to be moved this time.

Each had to strike work till the Authorities would tire of punishing us. Those who had a limited term to do were sent down to the Magistrate's court for a trial, while Mr. Lowis, the Deputy Commissioner, was to sit in judgment over us. The day before that of the trial, Mr. Lowis came to make some enquiries about the strike.

We told him all about the treatment we had had. He said, "You see, we go by the orders of the Government of India, and have absolutely no hand in the affair. The Government does not like to treat you better than ordinary convicts."

"But we don't get as much. If an ordinary convict is literate, he is given an easy job; if he is not, he may be a warder, or a Petty Officer. But we have no such chance. Others get 12 annas a month after 5 years, and can support themselves after ten years; but we have got to rot in the jails for all the time to come."

"Yes, I know. But all this is as the India Government orders."

Then you have no powers given you to do some good? All that the Government allows you is to whip us to the heel?"

Mr. Lowis laughed and said, "But one must maintain the jail discipline."

"That is, you are to keep up this fetish of a discipline at all costs, even if it means blatant injustice?"

He did not reply to this, for he knew too well what the real situation was. But as a servant of the Government he had to punish us as it seemed proper. We met him once more later on, and had a talk with him. When it came to Ullaskar, this man said of Ullas, "He is one of the noblest boys I have ever seen; but he is too idealistic." Yet the exigencies of service compelled him to punish the same Ullas.

But all sorts of penalisation was unequal to the maintenance of discipline. The common convicts followed us and struck. The jail works suffered considerably till the Authorities had the good sense to see that something must needs be done.

Then suddenly some seven or eight of the term-convicts were repatriated, and the jailor who had never been tired of reviling us came to us like a harmless gentleman and said, "Give your strike up. You can now retreat with honour." We did not know why he adopted the conciliating tone. Possibly he had had an inkling of the Government resolution of repatriating the term-convicts and introducing some amelioration for those who remained over. However, we agreed, and said, "All right. But some change must take place in three months. Otherwise we shall hoist our flag again."

So a scrap of a paper secured peace between the parties, and the second chapter of the strike episode was somehow satisfactorily closed.

CHAPTER XIII

THE TERMS that we were offered were:
(a) That we would have to work in the jail for fourteen years;
(b) That after that period we would be allowed to go outside the jail, and would be excused prison labour.
(c) That we could cook our own food inside the jail, and could dress ourselves like all outdoor convicts, that is, we could have dhoties, shirts and long turbans instead of jangias, skull-caps and sleeve-less jackets.
(d) That ten years of good behaviour which meant no sort of strikes or splits with the Authorities would make the Government reconsider our case with a view to further concessions.

We could not clearly see the advantage of all these terms, but we were so glad to be allowed to do our own cooking, and saved from hard grinding.

Barindra was placed in charge of the cane factory; Hemchandra became a Librarian, while I got to manage the oil-crushing department. As the two hours allotted for our meal were insufficient for doing the cooking, we used to take only rice and dal from the regular common kitchens, and cooked the other dishes for ourselves.

The Big Brother was a famous expert in the culinary art. As a matter of fact he was exceptionally good at preparing dishes of meat, polao, and such other things as might do justice to the table of a Nawab. But so far as it regards the cooking of ordinary things he did not rise much above us. One day we got a flower of a plantain, and we wished to make a special dish of it as the Bengalee people do it at home. But none of us had an idea of the recipe. A conference was convened; but unluckily no two opinions agreed. Barindra said, "My grandma came off the famous Dutt's of Hatkhola (Calcutta) and was a ripping good cook. By all the known laws of heredity, I may claim to be in the right."

Hemchandra spurted out, "Nonsense! I spent lots of years studying culinary art in France. You must not question my recipe."

In all National enterprises it is fashionable to select men with foreign degrees and diplomas, so we had to submit to Hemchandra as the unquestionable authority. I sat down as his assistant and did the thing under his instructions. Item no. 1, some oil to be put in the pan; item 2, onions sliced up; item 3, the flower itself properly minced. At this stage I fairly came to suspect the genuineness of my friend's diplomas. The process was going straight against our old idea of the dish, and looked over-French. But Authority can never be questioned, and I had nothing to do but submit to it. When the thing was done, lo, it had strange looks and tastes! A shiny black thing thickly smacking of onions! At due time of the meal, it occasioned a roar of laughter. Barin remarked, "Look here, old fellow, you are a real chef-de-cuisine. My grandma could never have done anything like this." Hemchandra was ready with a repartee, "This has been the bane of your life, my boys, you simply idolise the rules your grandma made for you. Why don't you move out and strike new paths?' A few days after this, we had another of these kitchen problems. This time, it was about that special preparation known in Bengal as "sukta'. Opinions, as usual, differed hopelessly over the recipe. Hemchandra at last observed, "Brother it! Why, you put in an ounce of quinine into any dish, and you will get what you want." Our Bengali housewives who do this cooking business at home may well try this recipe. If it turns out successfully, it will be as good as God's blessing; for to a malaria-ridden people as the Bengalis are it may be used both as a tonic and a palatable dish to the eternal credit of our Big Brother.

For our cooking purposes we took some stuff from the common store and occasionally did some marketing. The Regulations allowed us 12 oz. of milk for which we had to pay partly. After that payment, we each got 4 as.[Annas] which was the only means of our living. Then when a printing house was set up in the jail, Barindra was its manager; and Hem also got a lift as the manager of the Book-Binding Department. The superintendent applied to the Chief Commissioner for allowing them Five Rupees a month. But the application apparently staggered the great officer. A convict to get Five Rupees a month! Why, that meant that the Government would do well to head straight for clear bankruptcy. So he could not but decline. After a lot of petitioning followed by much of recommendation from the superintendent, these lucky "convicts got an astonishing allowance of one rupee a month. "Better something than nothing"—as the proverb goes.

In time there grew up a small kitchen garden by our cook-shed, and startled the jailor with the novelty of the thing. He would have come to enforce the discipline at our cost; but for the kind Superintendent, who said, "These fellows do not give you any trouble. Why not let them alone?" The Superintendent had some mighty reasons to get unusually kind. The brave exploits of the Authorities suffered a cruel exposure in the Indian papers in spite of all they could do to confine them to the precincts of the jail. The publicity had at first infuriated them; but very soon they chanced to find out that no good was to come out of playing the tyrant with us. Then there was the Great War that also softened the tempers of our "Governors." Shortly after the outbreak of the War, they looked anxious and relaxed in their zealous care of the convicts. We, in the Andamans, had all the war news from the assassination of the Austrian Prince to the Central Powers' march up to within twenty miles of Paris. The common convicts only knew it when the 'Emden' had emptied its broadside on the Madras coast. An appreciable fall in the inland trade, that left a heavy stock in the jail industries, was also equally eloquent. The authorities also floated a War Loan in the jail, selling loan-bonds to the convicts. But these people had no love for the British, whom they always regarded as their worst persecutors, and all the hands were raised in praying for a German victory. Somebody circulated that the Kaiser had ordered a general release, and soon a host of prophets appeared on the scene. One assured us that a famous Pir Saheb had clearly predicted the overthrow of the British in 1914; and another that a prophecy to that prospect had all along been found in the sacred books. From daybreak to sundown, this was the only topic of the jail; and the orderlies of the Governors themselves carried wonderful tales to accentuate the ill-feelings of the convicts.

This mentality of the convicts, which far from being friendly, was soon found out by the Authorities and the Superintendent lent us copies of the London Times so that we might not doubt the unbroken victories of the brave allies. But the "Times" soon proved to be too much of a tax on our credulity. In a sudden access of curiosity, we once totalled up the daily advances of the Allies for some months together, and found that, according to the correct authentic reports of the London paper, the allies should by that time cover all the distance between France and Poland. But as a matter of fact, the fight was still confined to Flanders. We ourselves could not account for this obvious inconsistency; so how could we convince the common convicts who could never bear with us to tell them of British successes? They were further obsessed with the idea that the Governors were putting them off with bluffs.

At that time the influx of some new convicts set some strange rumours on. A party of these told us that they had heard from reliable sources in their country that the "Emden" had carried away all the political prisoners of Port Blair. They would not give up their opinions even when they found us present as solid physical facts. For India, authority has always been the stronger proof, stronger even than direct evidence; and these poor people would only keep to the tradition of their land. There were other reports equally interesting and instructive. The War had sent some rebel prisoners from the army in France or Mesopotamia, and these always managed to infuse the convicts with thrilling hopes. The new arrivals gave out that when Enver Pasha would face a gun, it would not go off; and that the same master of a thousand odd miracles had come over to India to arrange the establishment of a Pan-Islamic Empire. Some even went further to allege that the Kaiser had already accepted the creed of the Prophet. All these set the jail people dancing wild with joy; and it was never safe to contradict these wild reports. For ourselves we did our best to glean the truth from newspapers, and from the more reliable accounts of the Irish soldiers of the British Squads that had been brought in to look after some newly imported Sikh convicts. Then new convicts were always hailing from India, who let us have an idea of things here. We were told by some of these that a geographical chart of the Andamans had been found among other papers on board the "Emden". We did not know what the Germans intended to do; but they forced the Authorities to get some reinforcement in men and ammunition.

Among the new batches were some fifty of the "Ghadar" Sikhs, some men of the Sikh battalions charged with treason, and some sixteen of Bengalee political convicts. They swamped the jail as it were. Only four or five of these had to press oil, and the rest were put on coir-pounding. But the Sikhs soon found fault with the Regulation food.

They were all tall giants of men, come back from America, and used to meat dishes. So two tiny slices of bread and an apologetic quantity of rice were too little for them. Then they were not meek enough to patiently bear with the insults of the jail. In a little time, they came to collide with the precious Governors. The trouble began with Paramanand of Jhansi. He was dragged to the jailor on some charge and gave back the jailor more hard words than he got. From hard words they came to blows,—and as an upshot of this, Paramanand was flogged. This gave a hint for strike, which, however, fizzled out. The jailor himself promised to behave better in the time to come, and so managed to evade the strike.

But the fire smouldered, and flared up in a blaze shortly. Sundays were off-days for the convicts, and they did their washing on these days. But the Authorities set them weeding the grass of the jail compound or swabbing the buildings. So practically, it was a mere name. Jagatram, editor of the "Ghadar" (Mutiny) of American fame, and a few others protested against the official autocracy and refused to work. The Superintendent tried them, and sentenced them to six months of fetters and confinement. This was all out of proportion with the magnitude of the offence, and displeased all. They struck work. At this point, an old Sikh had a row with his warder and gave out that the latter had thrashed him in his cell.

God knows if it were true; but the man had dysentery very soon after this, and was removed to the Hospital where phthisis overtook him. It was not long before he died. The major portion of the convicts were impressed with the notion that the thrashing the warder had given him was the direct cause of the poor man's death. A few under the lead of Prithvi Singh protested and went on hunger-strike. They were kept alive on milk artificially pumped in. Prithvi Singh sustained this for five long months.

The horror of this thing might have raised thunder-storms in other lands, but in Port Blair it was an every-day affair of scarcely importance enough to interest a boy. Even the death of some ten or twelve convicts was no notable thing there. As a matter of fact, three or four of the Sikhs again caught phthisis and popped off. I have spoken of Pandit Ramaraksha before; he died at this time. Another Sikh grew quite desperate and got rid of the jail torments by swallowing a lump of lead.

But while the dead somehow or other got peace, those who were demented were more unfortunate. Jatischandra Pal was one of these latter. He went off his brains in his confinement. Later they sent him back to India, and he is still in the Berhampore Lunatic Asylum.

Events like this were too numerous to be recounted in detail. One scarcely remembers all the cases, and can do bare justice, to them within the scope of a volume like this. Life was all fire and brimstone in the hell there,—a hopeless fight against uncommon odds. But the case of Chhatra Singh is much too important to he passed over. He had been a teacher in the Khalsa College of Lyallpore. His offence must have been something unusual; for he was always a confined prisoner at Port Blair. When the strike of the Sikhs was going on in full swing, he one day got excited and assaulted the Superintendent. We never saw it though, but only had a hearsay knowledge. However, the warders gave him such a licking that he lost his senses and then they locked him up for some two years or more. A cage was built for him in a corner of a verandah, and he had to do all things there. This naturally well nigh killed him. Another Sikh, Amar Singh, had a similar fate.

When the mortality rate went up rapidly, the Authorities awoke to the seriousness of the situation. The strike was the only blessed fighting weapon of the weak and the Sikhs tried it again. But the leaders gave it up at the critical moment, and party spirit broke its back-bone. It was at this time that the

Great War ended on the blood-stained plains of Europe, and we in that horrible edge of the Earth sat in expectation of new things that God might send us.

CHAPTER XIV

THE SUPERINTENDENT would often discuss politics with us. But all his discussions were meant to sing the glories of the British, and the greatness of their Government. It is both polite and politic to accept the worse of a controversy to which a woman or an officer makes a party. But this piece of saving common sense could not always prevent us from giving him some bitter facts about the much-belauded British Government. One must give his tongue some liberty when it is the only means of easing the mind.

The Russian debacle had already set in when one day the jailor sent for us and asked, "I hear the Superintendent talks politics with you. What do you think he wants of you?"

I replied, "I can't say, sir. But I think he wants to sing the glories of his nation. Is there anything else behind it?"

"Yes. You know a half-yearly report of each of you is despatched to the India Government. The Superintendent takes note of your political views and uses the stuff for the reports. Things are in a hopeless mess now. But if the English lose the War, well, the matter ends there. But if they have the victory, mind you, they may let you off at the first impulse of joy. So have a care. I am an Irishman, and I know these English people more than you can ever hope to. It is not wise to give voice to your thoughts here in the jail."

I turned this over and over in my mind, and found they were all really true. The jail was certainly no public platform to deliver speeches from. We took his advice and put a check on the tongue. After that, whenever the Superintendent would talk on the War, and the villainy of the Germans, we at once stood by him and said that those savages of the Germans would be certainly pitched into the darkest hell, and have no chance of the happy Paradise in which the English had already had a purchase. Strange! This confounding bigotry of the British mind! A Britisher can seldom get beyond his particular selfish point of view. He always likes to be told that all the three hundred millions of Indian people are perfectly enamoured of British rule; and he never in his life entertains a doubt that this Government is as perfect a system as human brains can devise.

Yet it was a grim irony of Fate when this same Superintendent lost his faith in the Indian Government.

Poor man, he had worked hard during all the War- time, and substantially contributed to the War Funds by reducing the jail expenses; but when at the conclusion of the War, he applied for six months' leave to go Home with his only daughter, he was not granted it! He sent one application after another to no earthly purpose. At last, he said, "All Governments are bad. I am an anarchist", and wanted to resign. Once in a just access of anger he said, "The Gods of Simla are incorrigible." The very man had another time remarked in connection with the draft of the Montford Reforms—the draft that would leave the

India Government uncontrolled by popular opinion— 'It's all right. The Government of India are sensible people." But this is no wonder. None can know how others suffer unless his or her own interests get a shock.

Before the outbreak of the War, we had almost given up the hopes of ever getting our freedom. But with the end of the War, there were fresh talks about our release. A rumour of a general amnesty was thick in the air. It raked up old embers of a hope, and made our clays heavy. We even heard of a Government circular purporting to let off all political convicts not charged with section 302 of the I. P. C., and in their eighth year in the Andamans. A few days later, we were again told that the list of the convicts recommended for release contained our names, and that it now all depended on the sanction of the Bengal Government.

The annals of the Port Blair jail never showed that a political convict who had come out to do a life sentence there had ever returned home alive. Those who had come after the Mutiny of 1857 had died on the spot one after another. Some Burmese who had come from the War with King Thebo [Thibaw] were still living there. So we would hardly dare fancy that we would fare otherwise. But we clung to this with all the tenacity of a leech. It was our only means of life under the strong stress of a thousand emotions. Then in time, the Treaty was signed, and England celebrated the victory. Yet no news of our release. We had counted days into weeks, and weeks had rolled into months since the days of the Truce. The mind grew restless. But the papers told us that India would celebrate the victory in October. So, there was yet one lingering ray of hope. October came and India did celebrate the victory! A tense anxiety seized us. When would the blessed news came? At last, it came. One day, the Superintendent summoned us to his office and told us that the Indian Government had been pleased to remit us one month in the year. Good Heavens! to see all our hopes lasted like the first budding flowers in an April frost. Then it was plain as a pikestaff that we had to rot in Port Blair for the rest of our lives. We resolved in that case to make the best of our time there. Accordingly, we at once submitted a petition to the Chief Commissioner to the effect that we should be exempted from prison labour as we had already done our stipulated fourteen years inclusive of the remissions. But the petition must have lost itself somewhere among the papers of His Honour's office. We never had a reply to it.

By that time the Jail Committee were to come to Port Blair. I decided to give these gentlemen a bit of my free mind and ease off the feelings that oppressed the heart. Then it would be best to resign ourselves to fate and let things drift as they liked.

But God meant to save us now. Some two days after the departure of the Jail-Committee, the Superintendent called on us and communicated to us the news that the Bengal Government had ordered us to be sent back to Alipore whence we would be released. We had no time to unveil the mystery which shrouded this sudden change of the official mind. But it made us mad with joy and excitement. Only one wise friend observed, "Patience, boys. Don't haloo till you are fairly out of this wood. The ship that takes you back may yet go splash down in the high seas." For the two days that lay in our way, the two days that separated us from the day which would see us leave off the cursed island, we lost sleep in the night and taste for all food. Imagination conjured up hundreds of visions.

Long forgotten faces flashed out from the depths of oblivion like the stars that drop out in the dark heavens. So, all those who had given us over shall get us once again in their loving circle!

The two dragging, tiresome, days were at last passed. We made a party of twenty-six, and walked out of the jail. Some had still the irons on, which clanked heavily, with every footfall. Outside the gates, we were all lustily cheered up by the Sikhs with loud cries of "Victory be to God!" Then they sang out, "O God, O the tenth Spiritual Guide, Thou madest a swallow swoop down on a hawk. We bow to Thee."

Yes, it was clearly the hour when the swallow should swoop down on the hawk. Our hearts beat time to the song and I said, "O thou future leader of India, O thou living image of God, I humbly bow down to thee across the waters."

As we boarded the ship, we took a last view of Port Blair. Those great immortal lines of Wordsworth came spontaneously in my mind, "What man has made of man."

The ship skipped over the blue waters and the mind flew before it. The former flew day after day and the latter worked every blessed moment of the day as we drew near the coastlands. Were not some lights twinkling before the eyes. Well, they were of the Sagor Island. What could it be yonder but the beautifully curved mouth of the fair silver-voiced Rupnarain river? Why, sirs, nothing else. Then we had not sunk in the middle of the voyage. That was clearly an idle fear. At last, the ship was berthed in the Kidderpore Docks.

We were landed and escorted to the Alipore jail under a Police Guard. The same jail was so much associated with our lives! We were reported to the Superintendent while the men of the Guard took charge of what we had. There was very little with us. We had given away all our books to the boys at Port Blair. There must be no more of a concern with letters in the future. The past experience had been enough. The rest of our lives we were determined to spend like honest illiterates. We would simply have our regular meals, and keep all the time to the bed, without worrying about how things go on. After keeping us in wait for about half an hour, the Superintendent came on. It was Saturday, and we thought that he would detain us till Monday next. But he asked, "I think you like to leave today. Have you got anywhere to go to in Calcutta?" We at once replied in the affirmative. Why, we would sleep in the streets, if there were no roof to shelter us.

They let off Hemchandra, Barindra and myself that night. But he had no blessed spot to go to. First, we called at the house of Mr. C. R. Das, to find him out. He was not there. Then we trod all the way to the house of Babu Satcowripati Roy, a Vakil of the High Court, and a friend of Hem. Barin and Hem took a fancy to stop there, while I decided to go back home to Chandernagore. There was train at 10-30 P.M. in the night and I meant to catch it. But out in the streets I lost my way. Calcutta was a new city to me, and it took me almost an age to reach the Howrah station. The train had already gone off. It was a tedious affair to walk back to Bhowanipore, and the mind refused to do it. I, then, thought of calling on my father-in-law's house at the northern portions of the Town. I started at once for it and reached the place at midnight. The house was sleeping, and nobody replied to my repeated calls. I, then, thought of tramping through the streets of the City all the happy night. A wave of a new joy ridged up against my heart. Was it not the very first free night in open air on the broad public thoroughfare after twelve long years? There were no jailor, no Petty Officer, not even a dog of a warder. The past slipped off from me like a heavy mantle in a blessed moment; the future yet stood before me hanging in the prospect. I felt really untrammeled, unfriended for the time being. But this sense of loneliness was not oppressive; and it was altogether unmixed with any regretful feeling. The mind was bathed in a placid joy.

From Shambazar I took the Circular Road to the Sealdah station. My shoes, a new luxury after twelve years, began to pinch me hard till they broke the skin. I pulled them off and put them in a bundle in the arm-pit. But a Policeman spotted the bundle, and kept me waiting to satisfy his curiosity with all the information of my whereabouts. At first, I thought of telling him directly that I had a ticket of leave; but on second thought, I with held myself. Had I not already paid dearly enough for telling the truth? So, I said, "I come from Kalighat and am going to the Sealdah station." The man inspected my bundle, and fixed me with a look for a few minutes. Then he asked: "You are an Oriya?" I kept myself from laughing out with much difficulty and replied gravely—"Yes."

He allowed me to move on, which I did! after salaaming to his dignity. I took a train and reached Shamnagar at 2 A.M. in the night. Thence I was ferried over the Ganges and landed in the neighbourhood of my home. It was then close on 3 A.M.; the small streets were muffled in solitude; and ther lamps were all burning like a phantom row of stars in the air. So it was that I reached my house. What changed looks it had!

I gave a few raps on a window, and called my brothers by

the names. In a little while a window was flung open and a woman's voice, all quivering with anxious delight, asked, "Who are you, please?" Through a second window my mother put the same question. Nobody would take it as a fact that the impossible had actually happened.

Gradually they stood the first shock of a pleasant surprise that agitated the entire house. Some little kids came crowding about me; they had yet sleep on their eyelids. I did not know a single face in the group. A small boy was looking at me from a distance. My nephew introduced him, "Your own child, uncle." I had left him not bigger than some eighteen months, and I found him back some thirteen summers old.

Once more I brushed up my doll's house, and went to live in it. O my God, thou who sittest at the helm of Life and Death, whither wouldst thou lead me on this time?

GLOSSARY

Alipur – Alipur or Alipore is a neighborhood in South Kolkata. In 1908 when the Alipore Bomb trial was being held, it served as the district headquarters for the 24 Parganas.

Amarkantak – Located in Madhya Pradesh, Amarkantak is also known as the *Teertharaja* or 'king of pilgrimages'. It is the meeting point of the Vindhya and the Satpura ranges. Rivers Narmada and Son originate here and flow in opposite directions. The forests surrounding Amarkantak contain a rich variety of medicinal plants.

Baghbazar – Baghbazar is a famous locality in Kolkata, West Bengal. Located on the banks of the Hooghly River, it has played an active role in the growth and development of Kolkata. It is famous for the Baghbazar Ghat and is also associated with Ramakrishna Paramhansa and houses the Ramakrishna Sarada Math.

Barindra – Barindra Kumar Ghosh (1880–1959) was an Indian revolutionary, writer, editor and journalist. He was the younger brother of Sri Aurobindo. He was one of the founding members of the *Jugantar* movement. As one of the masterminds of the Muraripukur Garden House Scheme, he was one of the prime accused in the Alipore Bomb Case. He was sentenced to life imprisonment and transported to the Cellular Jail in Port Blair.

Bhagavata – The Bhagavata Purana also known as Bhagavata is one of Hinduism's eighteen great Puranas (*Mahapurana*). Composed in Sanskrit by Veda Vyasa, it promotes *Bhakti* (devotion) towards Lord Krishna, an avatar of Lord Vishnu.

Bhawanipur – Bhawanipur or Bhowanipore is a historic premium locality in South Kolkata in West Bengal. It was an important centre of Bengal Renaissance. Today, it is a bustling region and home to many recreational places, banks, commercial buildings, and renowned educational institutions. Some of its notable residents included Netaji Subhash Chandra Bose, legendary actor Uttam Kumar, etc.

Bhupen – Bhupendranath Datta (1880–1961) was a revolutionary, sociologist and anthropologist. The younger brother of Swami Vivekananda, he was associated with Sri Aurobindo and the Jugantar movement. He also served as the editor of Jugantar Patrika. In 1907, he was arrested on charges of sedition and imprisoned for one year. After his release, he went to USA for his master's degree and joined the *Ghadar* movement in California, where he studied about socialism and communism. He later became associated with the Communist Party of India though he never formally joined the organization. He was a great scholar in various fields with many books and articles to his credit. He brought to light the social and mass aspects of Swami Vivekanand and Ramakrishna Mission, who advocated and worked for the well-being of people.

Bibhuti – Bibhutibhushan Sarkar (1890-1942) was an Indian revolutionary hailing from the town of Nadia in West Bengal. He was involved in numerous revolutionary acts like Deoghar Bomb Case, Narayangarh Bomb Case and was sentenced to ten years of rigorous imprisonment and transported to the Andamans.

Biren – Biren Datta Gupta (1889—1910), was a revolutionary hailing from Dhaka district in undivided Bengal, who was actively involved in revolutionary activities from a very young age. He was inspired by Jatindranath Mukhopadhyay, alias Bagha Jatin, to join a secret society during the Swadeshi movement. He was hanged to death for murdering Shamsul Alam, Deputy Superintendent of Police, the chief investigating officer in the Alipore Bomb Case.

Bleak House Chancery – Bleak House is a novel by Charles Dickens. It is the story of the Jarndyce family, who wait in vain to inherit money from a disputed fortune in the settlement of an extremely long-running lawsuit of Jarndyce and Jarndyce.

CR Das – Chittaranjan Das (1870–1925), also known as Deshbandhu (Friend of the Nation), was a prominent Indian freedom fighter and lawyer who remained a towering figure in Bengal politics till his death in 1925. He was actively involved in the activities of the Anushilan Samiti and successfully defended Sri Aurobindo in the Alipore Bomb Case. Besides his political persona, he was also an accomplished poet.

Chandernagore – Chandannagar, also known by its former name Chandernagore, is a city in the Hooghly district of West Bengal. Chandernagore was the first trading post on the eastern bank of the Hooghly River, set up by the French in 1696. It grew as a prosperous trading town under the governance of Joseph Francois Dupleix and was the second most important French settlement in India after Pondicherry. Indo-French architecture can be visible in the colonial period bungalows in the city.

Charles Perdy Lukis (1857-1917), Director General of Indian Medical Service (1910-1917, first editor of the Indian Journal of Medical Research. Spent most of his professional life in India.

Charu Chandra Ray Choudhury – Charu Chandra Ray Choudhury was a professor at Duplex Vidyamandir, Chandernagore, who inspired another revolutionary Kanailal Dutta to join the Indian freedom struggle during the agitations surrounding the partition of Bengal.

Chidambaram Pillay – Valliyappan Olaganathan Chidambaram Pillai (1872-1936), also known as Kappalottiya Tamizhan ("Tamil Helmsman"), was an Indian freedom fighter who took part in the Swadeshi Movement. He considered Bal Gangadhar Tilak his guru. It was Sri Ramakrishnananda of the Sri Ramakrishna Ashram who inspired him to think about breaking the monopoly of British shipping in the Indo-Ceylon waters. It was then that he founded an indigenous Indian shipping service (Swadeshi Steam Navigation Company) that plied between Tuticorin and Colombo and in doing so he successfully challenged the British monopoly. His political activism irked the British authorities and made them insecure. As a result, they levied sedition charges against him and he was given a sentence of two life imprisonments (Forty years) in 1908. Due to vehement protests and his deteriorating health due to prison atrocities, he was finally released in 1912. Later, he joined the Indian National Congress and remained its member till his death.

Chitrakut – Chitrakut or Chitrakoot is an important historic region which lies in the northern Vindhya Range, spread over the states of Uttar Pradesh and Madhya Pradesh. Chitrakoot Dham is a famous city and pilgrimage centre in the Chitrakoot District of Uttar Pradesh. It literally translates as 'Hill of many wonders'. According to the epic Ramayana, Sri Ram spent 12 years of his exile here. It is believed that the supreme Gods of Hinduism, (Brahma, Vishnu, and Shiva) also took incarnation here.

Conan Doyle – Sir Arthur Ignatius Conan Doyle (1859–1930) was a British writer and physician. He created the character of Sherlock

Holmes in 1887, on whom he wrote 60 stories. His body of work includes nearly 200 novels, short stories, poems, historical books and pamphlets.

Deoghar – Deoghar, also pronounced Devaghar is a city in Jharkhand. It is a sacred place associated with the Baidyanath Temple, one of the 12 *Jyotirlingas* of Hinduism. In ancient time, this place was believed to be very pious and picturesque. A prevalent story states that Sati's heart had fallen here when her dead body was dissected by Lord Vishnu with his *Sudarshan Chakra*.

Duff College – Duff College was located at the Jorabagan area in Kolkata. The college was established by Alexander Duff, a Christian Missionary, who founded the famous Scottish Church College as well. It is defunct now.

Dwijendralal – Dwijendralal Ray (1863–1913) was an Indian poet, playwright, and musician. Following the 1905 partition of Bengal, he joined the cultural movement to reunite the two new Bengali provinces. During this time he wrote several patriotic songs that are immensely popular even today. He composed over 500 Hindu mythological and nationalist historical plays and songs known as *Dwijendrageeti* or the Songs of Dwijendralal, thereby creating a separate subgenre of Bengali music.

Emden – The German light cruiser which bombed Madras harbour in September 1914. The bombing stuck the oil tanks belonging to the Burmah Oil Company and destroyed around 346,000 gallon of oil. The attack was made with the intention of crippling British trade in that region.

Enver Pasha – smail Enver, better known as Enver Pasha (1881–1922) was an Ottoman military officer and a convicted war criminal who was responsible for the Armenian Genocide during the First World War. He was also one of the organisers of the 1908 Young Turk Revolution.

Giridih – Giridih is a city in Jharkhand which is known for its industrial and health sectors as well as the Giridih Coalfield which is one of the oldest working coalfields in India.

Havildars – Havildar or Havaldar is an official rank in the Indian army, equivalent to a British Sergeant.

Hemchandra Das – Hemchandra Das Kanungo (1871–1951) was an Indian revolutionary who was a member of the *Anushilan Samiti*. A man of versatile qualities, he spent a few months in Paris where at the request of Shyamji Krishna Varma and Madam Kama, he designed the Indian National Flag for the first time. He was involved in the Alipore Bomb case and was sentenced to imprisonment for life and transported to the Andamans. In the Cellular Jail, his art of book-binding drew the admiration of one and all, including the notorious jailor Mr Barry, who assigned him the charge of the jail library. He was released in 1921.

Hotilal – Hotilal Verma was a freedom fighter hailing from Mathura in Uttar Pradesh. He served as the third editor of Swaraj newspaper, which was published from Allahabad and helped ignite the flame of independence throughout the country. For his anti-colonial writings, he was arrested in 1908 and later deported to the Andamans.

Hrishikesh – Hrishikesh Kanjilal was a revolutionary from Bengal who was involved in the Alipore Bomb Case and sentenced to life imprisonment.

Indu – Indubhushan Roy (1890-1912) was a young Indian revolutionary who was involved in the Alipore Bomb Case and convicted to 10 years rigorous imprisonment and deported to the Cellular Jail, Andaman. There he underwent unexplainable torture. Unable to bear the physical and mental torture, he committed suicide on 29 April 1912.

Inspector-General Plowden – Inspector-General CWC Plowden was the founder of the Criminal Investigation Department (CID), Bengal in 1906.

Inspector Samsul – Khan Bahadur Shamsul Alam was the Deputy Superintendent and Intelligence Officer in Bengal police who was murdered by Biren Dutta Gupta.

Indian Jail Reforms Committee 1919-1920 headed by Alexander Cardew, British civil servant, Member of the Executive Council of the Governor of Madras, Acting Governor of Madras between March and April 1919.

Jhusi – Jhusi is a town in Prayagraj district, Uttar Pradesh. It was formerly called Pratishthan Pur or Puri. It is a twin city to Prayagraj and is connected to it by the Lal Bahadur Shastri Bridge over the River Ganges.

Jyotishchandra Pal – freedom fighter, a close revolutionary aid of Jatindra Nath Mukherjee (Bagha Jatin), arrested during the Battle of Balasore on 9 September, 1914, Jyotish was tried and sentenced to transportation for life to the Cellular Jail. Historian Prithwindra Mukherjee writes, 'Unable to prove the complicity of Jyotishchandra Pal', the Counsel for the Crown, 'condemned him to transportation for life. Deported to the Andamans, he suffered a few years of inhuman moral and physical torture at the Cellular Jail where he met some of his old colleagues, sentenced in the Alipore Case… Upendranath Banerjee in his memoirs of the Andamans speaks of Jyotish. Half insane Jyotish was brought back to Bengal 'for a more kindly treatment at the Behrampore jail.' Shattered in physical and mental health' he died in jail on December 4 1924. (Prithwindra Mukherjee, *Bagha Jatin: Life in Bengal and Death in Orissa (1879-1915)*, 2016)

John Bull – John Bull is an imaginary figure who is a personification of England, similar to the American 'Uncle Sam'. In cartoons and caricatures he is shown as a prosperous farmer of the 18th century. He originated in satirical works of the early 18th century and stood for 'English liberty' as opposed to the revolutionaries.

Kalighat – Kalighat is a *Ghat* (landing stage) dedicated to Goddess Kali on the old course of the Hooghly River (Bhāgirathi) in Kolkata. The famous temple, Kalighat Kali Temple situated here is regarded as one of the 51 *Shakti Peethas*. It is the site where the toes of the right foot of Sati had fallen. The name Calcutta or Kolkata is said to have been derived from the word Kalighat.

Kamalakanta – Kamalakanta Bhattacharya (1769–1821), also known as Sadhaka Kamalakanta, was a noted Tantrik Yogi of Bengal in the late 18th century. From his childhood, he developed an interest in spirituality and later received initiation into Tantric Yoga from a Tantric Yogi named Kenaram Bhattacharya. He was a great devotee of Goddess Kali and composed numerous devotional love poems for the Goddess.

Kanai Dutta – Kanailal Dutta (1888–908) was an Indian freedom fighter and revolutionary who was renowned for his significant contributions to the Indian freedom struggle. He was a member of the Jugantar and involved in the Alipore Bomb Case for which he was arrested and lodged in Alipore jail. While the trial was going on, one of the revolutionaries, Narendra Goswami turned British approver. A plan was hatched to eliminate Goswami and Kanai Dutta along with Satyendra Bose murdered the traitor, for which they were both sentenced to death.

Khulna – Khulna is a major city in Southern Bangladesh. It is an industrial city situated on the banks of Rupsha (and Bhairav) River. It is also called the gateway of Sundarbans in Bangladesh.

Kidderpore – Khidirpur or Kidderpore is a locality in Kolkata, West Bengal. It served as the dock for the Port of Calcutta. It was from here that the ships carrying freedom fighters sentenced to 'transportation for life' used to leave for the Andamans.

Magistrate Kingsford – Douglas Kingsford, former Chief Presidency Magistrate of Calcutta was a colonial British judicial officer who dealt with a number of cases against freedom fighters and revolutionaries in his court. His judgments on Indian revolutionaries were not based on merit but on hate and partiality.

Manicktala – Manicktala or Maniktala is located in Kolkata, West Bengal. Some people are of the opinion that the area is named after the tomb of Manik Pir. But some attribute the name to one Manikchand Bose, the bodyguard of Aliwardi Khan, the Nawab of Bengal. The Muraripukur Garden House was located in Maniktala.

Montford Reforms – Montague-Chelmsford Reforms of 1918, which became the basis of the Government of India Act of 1919. The Act spoke of greater Indian participation in Government as a step towards the achieving of responsible self-government by Indians within the Empire.

Mr Barry – David Barry, the Jailor of the Cellular Jail in Andamans, was notorious for his insane cruelty.

Mr Birley – Mr Birley was the District Magistrate of the 24-Parganas district in the Indian state of West Bengal during British rule.

Muzafferpur – Muzafferpur or Muzaffarpur is a city located in Bihar. It is known for the assassination attempt on Magistrate Douglas Kingsford (Alipore Bomb Case) by two young Indian revolutionaries, Prafulla Chaki and Khudiram Bose in 1908.

Nalini Kanta Gupta – Nolini Kanta Gupta (1889–1984) was a revolutionary, linguist, scholar, critic, poet, philosopher and yogi, and among the most senior of Sri Aurobindo's disciples. He left a promising academic career and joined a small revolutionary group under Sri Aurobindo. He was involved in the Muraripukur Garden House Scheme and was arrested for the Alipore Bomb Case in 1908, but was acquitted a year later. After his acquittal, he worked as a sub-editor for the *Dharma* and the *Karmayogin*, two of Sri Aurobindo's Nationalist newspapers. In 1910, after Sri Aurobindo's retirement from politics, he and a few other disciples settled in Pondicherry and in 1926, the Sri Aurobindo Ashram was founded of which Sri Nolini Kanta Gupta became the secretary. The rest of his life was spent in Pondicherry, where he was involved in spiritual and scholarly works and here he breathed his last on 7 February 1984.

Nanigopal – Nani Gopal Mukhopadhyay (1895-1978) was a member of Jugantar. In February 1911, he was deputed to assassinate CID officer Denham but by mistake he threw a bomb in another car and was caught while he was trying to escape. During his trial, he was punished for 14 years and sent to Andaman Cellular Jail. He was later released in 1920.

Naraingarh – Naraingarh or Narayangarh is a major town in the Kharagpur subdivision of the Paschim Medinipur district of West Bengal. On 6th December 1907, Barindrakumar, Prafulla Chaki, and Bibhutibhushan threw a bomb made by Hemchandra Kanungo, on the train in which Lieutenant Governor Andrew Fraser was travelling. This event came to be known as the Narayangarh Bomb Case.

Narendra Gossain – Narendranath Goswami was a revolutionary who had turned British approver in the Alipore Bomb Case. He was murdered by Kanailal Dutta and Satyendra Nath Bose.

Nimtalla Ghat – Nimtalla Crematorium is located on Beadon Street,

Kolkata. The crematorium is also historically known as Nimtala Ghat. Among the famous personalities who were cremated here was Rabindranath Tagore.

Pandit Paramanand – Pandit Parmanand (1892-1982) of Jhansi was a freedom fighter, great patriot and renowned revolutionary. He was in prisons including Cellular Jail in Port Blair, Andaman Islands, for the longest period of nearly 33 years. His fiery speeches influenced the young and old alike.

Pandit Ramraksha – Pandit Ram Rakha (1884–1919) was an Indian revolutionary from Punjab and a member of the Ghadar party. He was known primarily for his involvement in the Mandalay Conspiracy Case in 1917, for which he was sentenced to life imprisonment in the Andamans. In the Cellular Jail he clashed with the prison authorities because he refused to submit to the humiliating conditions and opposed the inhumane treatment meted out to fellow prisoners. Prison officials attempted to seize his sacred thread. He was thrashed mercilessly by the officials who wanted to force him to submit. As a mark of protest, he went on a hunger strike. In such inhuman conditions, he passed away in 1919.

Prithvi Singh Azad – (1892–1989) was an Indian independence activist, socialist revolutionary, and one of the founder members of the Ghadar Party. He was attracted to the nationalist movement while he was still in his teens. He was influenced by the arrest of Lokmanya Bal Gangadhar Tilak and the sacrifice of Khudi Ram Bose. In connection with the Ghadar Uprising, he was arrested by the British on 7 December 1914. He was tried in the First Lahore Conspiracy Case and sentenced to death. The sentence was later commuted to life imprisonment in the Cellular Jail at Andamans. On 30 November 1922, while being transferred from Rajahmundry to Nagpur Central Jail, he escaped from the running train. He spent 10 years in various jails, including Calcutta, Madras, and the Cellular

Jail. He was a close associate of the famous revolutionary Chandra Shekhar Azad.

Professor Russell – He was a British professor at the Presidency College where he made some distasteful comments on Bengalis and was beaten up by Ullaskar Dutta.

Purna Lahiri – Rai Bahadur Purna Chandra Lahiri (1872-1942) was an Indian Police Officer during the British period. As an Inspector of Police, he arrested several leaders like Bhupendra Nath Dutta in 1907 and Sri Aurobindo in 1908 in connection with the Alipore Bomb Case.

Purushottam Natekar – Purushottam Natekar was a revolutionary from Satara in Maharashtra.

Rewa State – Rewa State, also known as Rewah, was a Rajput princely state in Central India ruled by the Baghel Rajputs. Surrounding its eponymous capital, the town of Rewa is in modern day Madhya Pradesh.

Robespierre – Maximilien Robespierre (1758–1794) was a French lawyer and statesman who was the main architect of the 'Reign of Terror' (1793–1794) during the French Revolution, when major political prisoners were executed by the use of guillotine.

Sachindra Nath Sen – Sachindra Nath Sengupta (1892-1961) was a noted dramatist in the contemporary Bengali theatre and a journalist who was associated with the Anushilan Samiti and took an active part in the Swadeshi movement.

Sandhya – Sandhya was a nationalist newspaper started in Bengal during the early twentieth century. It advocated nationalist and revolutionary ideas. Brahmabandhav Upadhaya served as its first editor.

Satyen – Satyendra Nath Bose (1882–1908) was a revolutionary who was associated with the Anushilan Samiti. His name first appeared in police records in the Midnapore Arms Case, when he was caught possessing an unlicensed gun and subsequently served two months in jail. He played an active role in the Nationalist movement in Bengal. Distantly related to Sri Aurobindo, he is most famous for an act of nationalism that ultimately nullified the legal threat posed to Sri Aurobindo and others. This was in connection with the Alipore Bomb Case where he and Kanailal Dutta murdered the fellow revolutionary turned British informer Naren Goswami who was supposed to present evidence against Sri Aurobindo. He was tried and executed for the same, along with Kanailal Dutta.

Shambazar – Shambazar or Shyambazar is a major locality in north Kolkata, West Bengal. It used to be the citadel of Bengali aristocracy, a part of what was earlier known as *Sutanuti*. It is believed that Shyambazar was named after Lord Krishna, who is also known as Shyam. The name is supposed to have been conferred upon the area by Sobharam Basak, a wealthy man in the 18th century.

Sir Andrew Fraser – Sir Andrew Henderson Leith Fraser (1848–1919) was a British officer of the Indian Civil Service and the Lieutenant Governor of Bengal between 1903 and 1908. He was also elected President of The Asiatic Society for 1905–07. An attempt was made by Bengal revolutionaries to assassinate him in the Alipore Bomb Case of 1908.

Sir Reginald Craddock – Sir Reginald Henry Craddock (1864–1937) was a British colonial official and politician who served in the Indian Civil Service and as Lieutenant Governor of Burma.

Sree Chand – Sree Chand or Sri Chand (1494–1629) was the eldest son of Guru Nanak, and founder of the Udasi sect of ascetic Sadhus. He established many *Akharas*, some of which being Akhil Bharatiya

Akhara Parishad and Shree Panchayati Akhada Bada Udasin.

Sudhir – Sudhir Sarkar (1889-1974), close revolutionary associate of Sri Aurobindo, Sudhir would often accompany Sri Aurobindo on his political tours and also undertake political missions on behalf of his leader, was sentenced to transportation to the Cellular Jail in the Alipore Bomb Case. Sudhir joined Sri Aurobindo Ashram in 1938 where he lived till his death in 1974.

Sukta – a popular Bengali dish consisting of vegetables and other condiments, slightly bitter in taste.

Sushil Sen – Sushil Kumar Sen (1892–1915) was a revolutionary from Bengal. He was involved in the famous Alipore Bomb Case and was arrested in May 1909. He was sentenced to seven years rigorous imprisonment which was later cancelled by the Calcutta High Court on account of scarcity of evidence.

Swami Pragnananda – Born as 'Devavrata', Swami Pragnanda was a renowned *Sanyasi* who also held the office of the President of 'Ramakrishna Vedanta Math' in Calcutta. He was a scholar par excellence and possessed knowledge on innumerable subjects. His contributions to the spiritual world always shined as a beacon of light for the seekers of truth. Many scholars have received their PhD and D Litt Degrees for Universities under his research guidance.

Swami Sarupananda – Swami Swarupananda (1871–1906) was a direct monastic disciple of Swami Vivekananda and the first president of the Advaita Ashrama, set up by Vivekananda in 1899 at Mayavati, Uttarakhand. He also doubled up as the editor of Prabuddha Bharat until his passing in 1906.

Thibaw Min (1859-1916) – Last King of Burma, was defeated by the British in the Third Anglo-Burmese War in 1885, he was exiled in Ratnagiri in Maharashtra.

Ullaskar – Ullaskar Dutta (1885–1965) was an Indian revolutionary associated with Anushilan Samiti and Jugantar, and was also a close associate of Barindra Nath Ghosh. When the Swadeshi Movement was at its zenith, Ullaskar gave up foreign clothes and adopted the traditional Bengali attire. In the year 1908, he was put behind bars on charges of his involvement in the Alipore Bomb Case. The explosive – devised to cause a blast on the railway track near Midnapur to derail the train and thus kill Andrew Fraser (the then Lieutenant Governor of Bengal) – was said to have been devised by him. He was sentenced to death in 1909. He filed an appeal against the death sentence and thereafter it was commuted to transportation for life. He had to undergo numerous atrocities in the Cellular Jail, causing him to lose his mental balance. He was released in 1920.

Upadhaya Brahmabandhav – Brahmabandhav Upadhyay (1861–1907) was a journalist and freedom fighter. He was a classmate of Swami Vivekananda and a close acquaintance of Gurudev Rabindranath Tagore. Hailing from Khanyan in Hooghly district of West Bengal, he was initially a Brahmo Samajist and afterwards converted to Christianity. However, under Swami Vivekananda's influence, he retraced his steps back to Hinduism. In order to propagate *Vedanta* in the West, he went to England where he gave a series of lectures on Hinduism. He founded the *Sarasvata-Ayatana* in Calcutta in the tradition of the Vedas. He actively supported Rabindranath's ideal of a Brahmavidyalaya and helped to organize the school in its early stages.

Vindhyachala – Vindhyachala is a city in Mirzapur district of Uttar Pradesh. The city is a popular Hindu pilgrimage site having the temple of *Maa Vindhyavasini*, who according to Markandeya Purana had incarnated to kill the demon *Mahishasura*.

Yugantar – Jugantar or Yugantar was one of the two major secret revolutionary organizations in Bengal which fought for India's independence; the other being Anushilan Samiti. It was formed in 1906.

MANIKTOLLAH GARDEN HOUSE REVOLUTIONARIES

Upendra Nath Banerjee

Ullaskar Dutt

Sishir Kumar Ghose

Sudhir Kumar Sarkar

Sushil Kumar Sen

Asoke Chandra Nandy

Bal Krishna Hari Kane

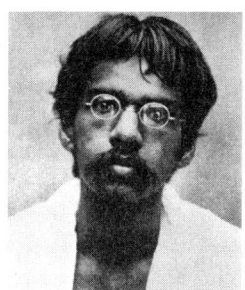
Barindra Kumar Ghose

Bibhuti Bhusan Sarkar

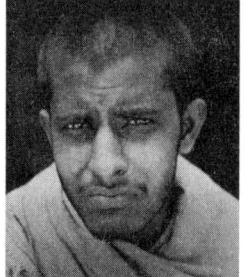
Bijoy Chandra Bhattacharjee

Bijoy Kumar Nag

Birendra Chandra Sen

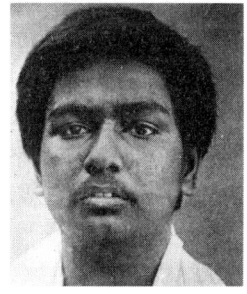
Birendra Nath Ghose

Debabrata Bose

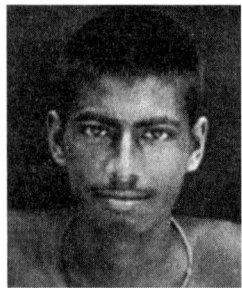
Dharani Nath Gupta

Din Dayal Bose

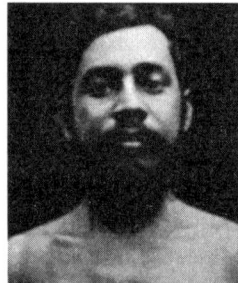
Hemendra Nath Ghose

Hrishikesh Kanjilal

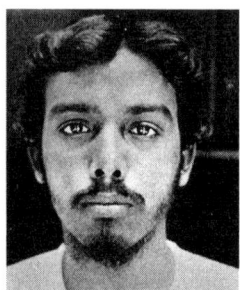
Indra Nath Nandy

Indu Bhusan Rai

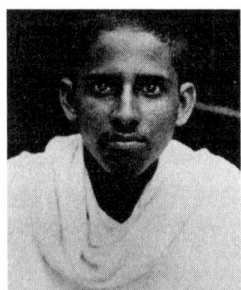
Krishna (Kristo) Jiban Sanyal

Kunja Lall Shaha

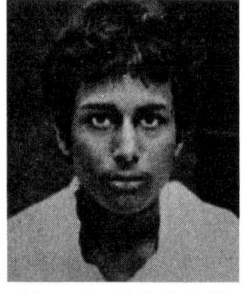
Narendra Nath Bakshi

 Nikhileshwar Roy Moulik

 Nogendra Nath Gupta

 Paresh Chandra Moulik

 Provash Chandra Deb alias Manik Lal Deb

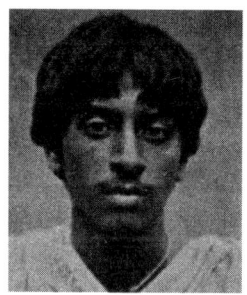 Purna Chandra Sen

 Sachindra Kumar Sen

Photo courtesy: Sri Aurobindo Ashram Archives, Puducherry